VISIONS AND AUTHORITIES

How the Church discerns her calling

Marjory A MacLean

Copyright © 2023 Marjory A MacLean

All rights reserved.

ISBN: 9798866723065

CONTRIBUTORS

Chapter 1B Rev Andy Braunston,
Minister for Digital Worship
United Reformed Church

Chapter 2B Rev Scott Rennie
Minister of Crown Court, London

Chapter 3B Rev Fiona Smith
Principal Clerk, General Assembly

Chapter 4B: Rt Rev Graham B Usher
Anglican Bishop of Norwich

Cover photo: the ceiling of Abernyte Church, Perthshire

VISIONS AND AUTHORITIES

CONTENTS

	Introduction	v
1A	Missio Dei, Missio Ecclesiae	1
1B	*Contribution by Andy Braunston* *Musings on Mission in the United Reformed Church*	18
1C	Church Without Walls	28
2A	Corporate Discernment	42
2B	*Contribution by Scott Rennie* *How can we tell? Discerning our calling together*	58
2C	Filling a Vacancy	64
3A	Semper Reformanda	80
3B	*Contribution by Fiona Smith* *'A Big Beast'*	96
3C	Organised Religion	102
4A	Bearing Authority's Burden	115
4B	*Contribution by Graham Usher* *Shepherds of Christ's Flock –* *Episcopal Authority in the Church of England*	131
4C	Power in the Congregation	140
5	From Scapegoat to Shibboleth	153
6	Sermon at an Induction	162
7	Sermon at an Ordination	166

ACKNOWLEDGMENTS

Thank you to Alison and Susan, Principal and Vice-Principal of New College in early 2023, for inviting me to offer the Short Course 'Navigating the Church's Mission'.

And thank you to Andy, Scott, Fiona and +Graham for being my willing co-operators in this little project.

INTRODUCTION

In 2010 the full-time role of Depute Clerk of the General Assembly was made redundant for a few years, and at the age of 47 I found myself facing a career-break. While waiting for a period of mobilisation in the Royal Navy to begin, I indulged my emotions in a collection of honest and cathartic essays published as *Speaking from the Heart*[1]. It is no longer in print, and I am grateful to the publisher for allowing me to re-use some of its material now, updated to reflect the turbulent half a generation that has passed since that moment.

In 2022 the first cohort of New College Fellows was activated by the Principal and Vice-Principal[2] as some of us were challenged to deliver in 2023 'Short Courses for Church People'. This coincided with another release of time and capacity in my diary, as I moved from full-time working to three-quarter stipend. So rather than aiming to deliver only the four seminars of the course I'd promised on the church governance elements of mission development, I decided to produce a new collection of materials and make it available through Kindle Direct Publishing

---

[1] Shoving Leopard, 2010
[2] Rev Profs Alison Jack and Susan Hardman Moore

for course members and other Church people alike who might find it provocative. There is no need to have attended the course before reading this book, which should contain everything you need to follow the themes of the discussion we enjoyed.

This is not an academic work. It comes with the assumption that those who would want to be academically qualified in ecclesiology will have studied it on a proper course during their ministerial formation. Other readers, not needing a scholarly approach, should find the texts here are accessible to the thoughtful non-theologian. No, it is meant rather to be a polemic, an irritant, a generator of debate and opinion, the kind of book that has always been written by academically-rusty parish ministers who know stuff they think the Academy does not.

The title *Visions and Authorities* will immediately resonate with readers of the Orcadian theologian John Oman whose book-titles often expressed difficult tensions[3] and included *Vision and Authority, or the Throne of St Peter*.[4] The nod to Professor Oman is a nod from me to Orkney (especially my former parish of Stromness in whose church John Oman came to faith), and to Principal Ruth Page who mentored many ministers, especially women of my generation, and whose professional failures included her vain efforts to persuade me to do my PhD on Oman's theology.

There are four overall sections corresponding with the four seminars of the Short Course delivered in the autumn term of 2023. Within each of those sections there are three pieces, and I have set the chapter headings in different fonts as follows, to indicate the source of each essay:

---

[3] Titles included: *Grace and Personality* and *The Church and the Divine Order*
[4] 2nd edition, London: Hodder and Stoughton 1928

- A new **lecture** addressing the main theme of the seminar
- An **introduction** from the guest contributor assisting with each seminar
- A revised version of an *essay* from Speaking from the Heart *which illustrates the overall theme from the recent history of the Church*

At the end of the book, as a 'bonus' item not used during the Short Course, I have presented a slightly revised version of one essay originally offered to the limited readership of the Affirmation Scotland Facebook page. I think it obliquely exemplifies some of what the other essays describe, especially in relation to questions of discernment and authority. Finally come two sermons preached at the outset of periods of (other people's) Christian service.

I am delighted to be able to include contributions – tantalisingly brief ones from people so busy – from the four adventurous souls who trusted me to include them in this process of stirring. Their involvement with this does not imply the slightest agreement with any of my notions and arguments, but their own thoughts will make the reader's engagement much the richer.

If the course, and this book, have an intellectual arc, it is an unforgiving examination of:

1. the particular corporate presbyterian process by which the Church of Scotland has come to its current subjection to a concept of 'mission', especially 'the Five Marks of Mission', that determines the direction of its resource-planning
2. the general corporate presbyterian process by which the Church of Scotland comes to any concept of what it should be doing about anything
3. the ways in which change ought to happen, does happen, doesn't happen, within the organism that is Christ's body

4.   the practical presbyterian processes by which we actually do anything, and how to make the best of them

The first of these may strengthen the arms of those who want to ask intelligent questions about current assumptions as the Church gropes its way into its Presbytery-Mission-Plan-shaped future.

The second might give some glimmer of hope to those who wonder whether there is any correlation between the action of the Holy Spirit and the action of the Church of Scotland.

The third might be useful to those who have a passion to improve things but want to be sure they won't just perpetuate the stuff that doesn't work.

The fourth would, dare I suggest, make worthwhile initial reading for those undertaking the Church Law element of ministerial formation.

Anyway, I'll leave it all here and hide in my preferred corner of the map where you can't find me.

M.A.M.

1A MISSIO DEI, MISSIO ECCLESIA

This lecture has two purposes.

The first is to consider the term 'mission' for its own sake, to trace its career in the modern lexicon of the Church of Scotland, and to critique the Church's reliance on a rather badly-defined version of mission in the ghastly experience – ghastly through no particular fault – that was the initial Presbytery Mission Planning process of 2021-22.

The second purpose, visible between the lines I hope, is to reflect on the threat to Church life that exists when well-intentioned and intelligent people have to rush at a financial emergency and respond by placing a very big decision on too light a conceptual foundation.

To put it bluntly, the Church of Scotland is currently restructuring its heritable, moveable, and human assets using a concept of 'mission' as the measure of everything it does. All over Scotland Presbyteries have written Mission Plans, and these contain biting creative ideas, acres of meaningless pulp, painful necessities and admirable ambitions. In some places it will be all people can do to implement the 'legal' bits, the restructuring, and the words about 'mission' will fade on the page. In some places the re-structuring will be done so well that people will feel they are being more 'mission-centred' than they were before. In some places, including where I live, the structural and the mission-development strands are given to different specialists to implement in the hope of keeping the best of everything.

What, then, is the problem?

Mission: the Church's problem word

What is mission? I don't mean that as an intellectual question, a starting-point for a scholarly debate about semantics or history or theology. I mean that as a plain question I have often asked, internally or out loud, in the middle of meetings or when listening to passionate churchy debates. It's clearly something you're supposed to prioritise, to understand, to exercise, or you don't pass the test for being a proper Christian. And yet the older I get, the more I feel like the little boy who saw the Emperor was naked; and when I challenge trusted friends to tell me what on earth mission is, they often surreptitiously confess they're not terribly sure, either.

Trust me, I have no problem with personal evangelism, with the Church's prophetic calling, with the developing of believers' discipleship and apostleship, or with the ushering in of God's promised Kingdom. My problem is with the noun 'mission', so difficult to define and then so aggressively brandished as a badge of virtue. Scholarly lifetimes are spent on this issue, and the results are complicated and profound. But the slightest scratch of the surface reveals that there is no single obvious 'thing' behind the label.

In the Bible, both in the adventure stories of Hebrew history and in the narratives of the earliest Church, 'mission' is always preceded by 'a' or 'the' or 'our', and it always describes a particular event – usually a journey with a purpose – undertaken by someone at someone else's behest. Whatever it is that people in the modern Church mean by 'mission' without either the definite or indefinite article, as some sort of generic concept of activity, *there is no such use in the biblical texts.* I can see how the word 'mission' has been chosen for that modern concept, because 'journeying with a purpose on someone's instructions' is a great *metaphor* for this way of being and believing and doing. But it is a metaphor; we do not find in the Bible a direct application of this word in the way we use it now.

Jesuits often claim to be the originators of the modern use of the term to mean the whole over-arching endeavour of an institution or life or calling.[5] After the Reformation, religious organisations beginning with the Society of Jesus would understand themselves to have a distinguishing purpose: an Order with a 'mission' to serve the poor, a Protestant society with a 'mission' to evangelise foreign countries during the colonial era. Eventually the usage seeped into the secular world, and businesses and academic institutions have mission-statements in varying degrees of vacuity (but that's up to them). This, though, is getting closer to the feel of the term as it's used in our Church today.

In an effort, presumably, to rescue the word 'mission' from such sector use by bits of the Church and instead to emphasise something the whole Church should be doing, a major conference of the International Missionary Council at Willingen, Germany in 1952 popularised a sudden revival of an old term *missio Dei* to

---

[5] O'Malley, JW, 'Mission and the Early Jesuits', in *The Way*, Supplement 79 (1994): 3–10

attribute that over-arching and still undefined meaning of mission to God. Ancient use of *missio Dei* by St Augustine and others referred to the part of trinitarian doctrine that describes the Father sending the Son and sending the Spirit, in the literal meaning of *missio*. After Willingen, there was an idea that whatever a general concept of mission is, it is a quality of the Divine not of the human, which had the effect of sanctifying the term in the vocabulary of the Church – which of course is always a good way to strengthen something that is otherwise a weak concept. What can it mean though? The 'mission of God' either means God *sending* something or someone from Godself, which does not take us beyond the Augustinian use of the word to refer to the sending of the Son and the Spirit, or it means Godself being *sent*, which makes no sense. Perhaps it does refer to something, something that is different from the Church's mission, *missio ecclesiae* – but has our denomination really found such a difference in its uses of the terms? Does talking about *missio Dei* really tell us anything? To answer that, it will be necessary to have an idea what this neologism 'mission' covers.

Mission: what it might involve

Here is a little list of things the Church's mission has been taken to mean.[6] The accuracy of the list is less important, for my argument, than the fact that there is such variety in what this one term might be taken to mean. It is the inability of the Church to agree a single definition that is the problem when so much weight is put on that word for such far-reaching structural decisions.

---

[6] This is a simplified and consolidated version of several lists contained in McKinzie, G 'Perspectives on *mission ecclesiae*: A Review Essay' in *Missio Dei* MD 9.2 (2018) at https://missiodeijournal.com/issues/md-9-2/authors/md-9-2-mckinzie

For some, when the Church uses the word 'mission' it must be meaning the element of its activities that could also be called **prophecy**, when it is the activity of the Church speaking God's truth to the world. This is a meaning close to that original biblical sense of being sent with a particular message to tell it to particular ears on behalf of a particular sender. It is a position that requires the courage to discern what God wishes to say, to arrive at a confidence that the discernment is true, and then the further courage to say those things that other people do not want to hear and to be resented for it. The prophecy may be to the powerful of the world (about creation, or justice, or power itself); it may be addressed within the Church (about purity, or inclusion, or change); it may be addressed to an individual (about commitment, or grace, or truth). It may be the least attractive way of being the Church, and perhaps it is the oldest.

For example, when COP26 took place in Glasgow in 2021, the churches sent high-level delegations to support the many voices of those campaigning for drastic measures to be taken to reduce the rate of global temperature increase. On one view of this effort and presence, it might seem as if those representatives were doing only what the representatives of environmental charities, local authorities and scientific institutions were doing, arguing a case on behalf of nature and suffering humanity, with no distinctive religious element. On another view of it, the churches were exposing their hypocrisy, clutching their pearls over climate change while failing to provide justice for victims of clerical abuse or root out conversion therapy disguised as spiritual advice. On a positive view, though, these conveners and bishops and theologians were exercising a ministry of prophecy, speaking on the Creator's behalf to those holding the power to save or destroy that Creation. And in those weeks, there was nothing more important the Church could have been doing; that was our mission then.

For some, including many readers of Barth, when the Church uses the word 'mission' it must be meaning the element of its activities that could also be called **translation**, rendering the Word of God audible and comprehensible to its hearers in the world; it's what we preachers are trying to achieve week by week. It's the dangerous and controversial work of wrestling with the authority and interpretation of the Bible, trying to keep the balance between the eternal message and its contemporary implications, and saying all of that convincingly and clearly and helpfully. It is about the tension between timeless truth and historical relevance; it's the hermeneutical task of showing how universal is the human condition and therefore how universal is the power of the Gospel message spoken into that condition. And it involves going to places we would not instinctively seek out (chaplains are good at this) where the Word needs to be translated into specialist language or colloquialism.

For example, when a new sailor or officer joins the Royal Navy, it's not just a new job but a new language and culture that must be learned. The vocabulary is so distinct (Jackspeak) that it has its own glossary, for terms that are acronyms (eg SOLAS[7]) or re-purposed (eg flat[8]). The culture is even more fascinating and takes years to assimilate. The exact status of trust and respect held for a very experienced Senior Rate (equivalent of Army NCO) by an intelligent junior officer almost defies description. The fact that most personnel would trust what a colleague said if they added the word 'safeguard', more than if they swore on the Bible, probably makes no sense to civilians.[9] The Naval Chaplain

---

[7] Saving of Lives at Sea

[8] the part of a passageway that opens out to create a useable space between compartments

[9] The Safeguard Rule is used during exercises where a fictional scenario is being played out. If the word 'safeguard' prefaces a broadcast pipe, it refers to a real situation not part of the fiction. It's like 'Simon says...', except you obey all the commands, but you do know when the fire in the engine compartments is

who can move naturally inside that culture, and can accurately converse in Jackspeak, has a chance to translate credibly the claims of the Gospel upon the lives of the Ship's Company.

For some, often in evangelical traditions, when the Church uses the word 'mission' it must be meaning the element of its activities that could also be called **individual transformation**, the profound conversion of life through a moment of change. Depending on your theological background that might be for soteriological motives (avoiding wrath, facing judgement) or participatory ones (joining in with the community of those following in the Way). With this understanding, the other definitions in this lecture might seem a foolish waste of time; mission as programmatic outreach to individuals to effect major spiritual change will be for some such an obvious definition that they would be puzzled that anyone could see anything else as more central or important.

For example, when a preacher's sermon is exploring the story of Saul's conversion on the road to Damascus, the congregation may conceal someone who has arrived at a sliding-doors moment in their own journey. Unbeknownst to those sitting around them, unbeknownst to that preacher, this individual may be facing a choice they can't ignore, a big one, a moral one. For reasons to do with health, or a relationship, or work, or past behaviour catching up with them, they are going to have to decide which way to move next: towards self-absorption and self-defence, or towards whatever they deeply hold to be virtuous that requires a very different decision. Saul's story may in that moment give that hearer ears to hear the right call, may give an example of opting for the larger, better life, may bolster courage to do the more noble thing. And who can do anything but admire

---

actually the real thing. If you think a sailor is telling you a tall tale, say 'Safeguard?'; and if they reply 'Safeguard' you can stake your life on its truth, because it's a matter of honour not to abuse that system.

those who feel called to bring as many people as possible to that *kairos* instant with every ounce of their Christian commitment?

For some, especially in higher catholic traditions, when the Church uses the word 'mission' it must be meaning the element of its activities that could also be called **sacramental participation**, the act of including people in the mysteries of the faith through its most symbolic worship. To a low-church Protestant, this is perhaps the least obvious focus of mission. To a cradle Catholic however, perhaps nothing could be more natural. Progress into a depth of personal faith is made in steps constituted by the sacraments and ordinances of Baptism, First Communion, Confirmation, Confession and so on. Without the structure these give to personal discipleship and piety, that sense of journeying in a clear direction is lost.

For example, at sea in the middle of the Mediterranean in a Royal Navy frigate, I planned a communion service for those few, those very few, in the Ship's Company who might wish to take part in the Lord's Supper. The concept of an open table is, naturally, at its most extremely 'open' in an environment where those of different denominations are literally unable to access sacramental worship in their own traditions. They just have to make do with what's on offer in the Junior Rates Dining hall during the dog watches next Sunday. When a Roman Catholic sailor came to talk to me, fairly sure she wasn't supposed to receive mass in a Protestant service, it felt like a significant moment – it felt, frankly, like a moment of mission – to be able to reassure her that this was the exception that was open to her (and anyway, who but Jesus was going to know?).

For some, perhaps especially in more liberal circles, when the Church uses the word 'mission' it must be meaning the element of its activities that could also be called **kingdom-building**, drawing men, women and children in to a common project beyond any individual focus. Whatever self-consciousness one person may have of their own salvation, spirituality, growth or healing, the work they do in the life of the Church is focused outwards to the needs of community and society; so I am 'working out' not *my* salvation but *ours*, quietly trusting that mine will be caught up in ours in due course.

For example, those Church representatives at COP26, or the faith representatives in local authority education committees, or mission partners creating sanctuaries in places of conflict, or the work-party from a Scottish congregation building a school in Malawi, or the staff of Crossreach creating an atmosphere of security for confused residents in care facilities; once again all of them are doing things others may do for motivations that have nothing to do with faith, and all of them are doing what they are doing *precisely* in service of the God in whom they have put their faith. They may labour to the advantage of human history, but they do so in pursuit of a vision greater than that.

Add to these categories, add to these stories, debate whether and how each really expresses the Church's mission. The point is that these are different things being put in the middle of different people's definitions of mission. Even within a single denomination we mean strikingly different things by the single word. And that matters when it's a word that we use so often and use as if we all knew what it meant - as if it meant only one thing. It just doesn't.

One solution for those who want mission to be the Church's one big thing is to say, 'it is all of these things, and other things, and it shouldn't be limited or narrowly defined'.

So, either this troublesome word 'mission' means the *whole* of what the Church does, or it refers to *part or parts* of what the Church does. (I'm assuming the reader and I are gracious enough to accept that it means *something*, so it must be one or other of those options.) To express that the other way round: either it includes all of Church life, or it excludes parts of Church life.

If it means the *whole* of what the Church does, the label 'mission' is not a term of discrimination that serves any purpose. It is then such a generic term that it has no function in making any distinctions amongst the many activities of the Church; it does not do anything to rank the importance of the sacraments and personal evangelism and community activism and pulpit-preaching because every one of those fits equally inside its definition. It is then too vague, too inclusive, to be used as a sharp instrument for making decisions and policies... and the radical re-structuring of a Church's assets.

It must, rather, be a term that specifies one or more *part* of the Church's activity, if it is to be used as the basis of a decision that has any substance or meaning. In assessing recent events in our Church, the question is: What definition *has* the Church used of 'mission', since we have seen that its meaning is not self-evident? What has been included? Conversely, therefore, what parts of the Church's life and work that do not come into our definition of the word 'mission' have consequently *not* been used as criteria for our recent big decisions? This, I think, is where the debate within the Church of Scotland is currently under way.

Marks of Mission and Marks of the Church

Into its legislation on the structuring of congregations and assets[10] the Church of Scotland has embedded a definition of

---

[10] Presbytery Mission Plan Act, Act 8 2021 as amended. https://www.churchofscotland.org.uk/__data/assets/pdf_file/0011/95987/2021-Act-8-Presbytery-Mission-Plan-Act.pdf

mission that adopts, adapts and confines itself to a fashionable Anglican summary called the Five Marks of Mission, in this formulation:

> *The mission of the Church is the mission of Christ: 1. To proclaim the Good News of the Kingdom 2. To teach, baptise and nurture new believers 3. To respond to human need by loving service 4. To seek to transform unjust structures of society, to challenge violence of every kind and pursue peace and reconciliation 5. To strive to safeguard the integrity of creation and sustain and renew the life of the earth.*

It would be a brave soul who would argue against the virtue and necessity of any of these five things. But there are voices raising questions about their sufficiency.

These five headings are just that, very general categories of activity with no specification anywhere (at least, not anywhere as authoritative as the legislation) to confirm what is included within each one. There's a mandate of proclamation in 1, and an indication is given in 2 of what to do with new believers. Where, though, is the critical moment that takes us from the first to the second, the moment of coming to faith, that *kairos* moment of transformation I mentioned? 4 and 5 are worthy statements of virtuous action that any caring atheist could agree with once the word 'creation' was translated into a more neutral term like 'nature'. What, though, constitutes the building of the Kingdom that has something to do with God?

There is insufficiency, then, in the meaning of what is contained in the list of the Five Marks. There is also insufficiency when you consider what is missing. Remember my argument earlier: if a definition of mission is to include the *whole* of what the Church does, then omissions from this list imply that it is a failure of a list. If, however, mission is only *part* of what the Church does, then this list does not fail on its own terms, but it cannot bear alone the full weight of the Church's structural decisions because there may be other things we should have taken into account.

An obvious alternative set of criteria might be the Marks of the Church favoured in several versions by the early Reformers. I have not resorted to those, because (1) there are different versions of the list, so they do not provide a universal standard and (2) they miss some of the items in the Five Marks of Mission, so probably do not take us any further. But some will prefer them as a more established measure.

Mission, worship and personal holiness

It has not taken long for no less a figure than the Convener of the Church's own Theological Forum, Liam Fraser, to point to a major omission from the catalogue of Church activities that should be used to make these important judgements: worship.[11] Fraser manages to conceptualise mission as emanating from God and Christ more easily than I do, but points out that mission then flows through the Church into the world. Logically therefore, and temporally, the Church must be constituted ready for that task, ahead of it. And what shapes the Church for this task, Fraser argues, is worship. It is in worship that the relationship of God with Christians is built, and there that we develop our resemblance to Jesus. Worship, according to this argument, is the workshop of the Lord.

'... *worship, teaching, and sacraments precede mission theologically, temporally, and practically, and mission is contingent on them. Mission is the fruit of abiding in Christ by the Spirit, and being tended and shaped by the*

---

[11] Fraser LJ, 'The Primacy of Worship and the Necessity of Mission: Some Reflections' *The Record*, Church Service Society 2022 vol 57 p33-43. Liam's article and this lecture, read together, are entirely consistent with each other, each expanding slightly different parts of the same argument.

Father. This abiding and shaping happens when we participate in worship both corporately and individually, and if we do not worship, mission will either fail to happen, become distorted, or peter out.'

In a way that the Five Marks do not, Fraser names the substance of Christian faith, its point and purpose, and answers the 'what for' questions that leave me wanting a lot more when I read the Five Marks. He is talking about something that happens between God and the human being, the 'something' that certainly is hinted at by the list of Marks but not described explicitly or adequately. He is describing the most precious experience, he is describing encounter with God, and it is hard to find that in Act 8 of 2021. Fraser, is, like me, interrogating the adequacy of the standard the Church has chosen to use in this painful area of its current thinking, and finding it wanting.

I would love to see him take the logical next step, in fact two steps, in his argument.

Fraser is arguing that worship is important as a precursor to mission; but since I am so unconvinced that the vague modern concept 'mission' really bears very close scrutiny, I would, as an immediate first step, want to strengthen and expand the statement to say, 'worship is important in the life of the believer and the Church', and avoid introducing the word 'mission' at this point. That encompasses much more. There is a palpable difference between an act of public worship that is constrained to serve the more common definitions of mission, and one that is not. Just as the definition of mission does not include the whole life of the Church, so therefore mission-centred worship fails to connect with areas of Church life or individual experience that happen not to fit inside that congregation's cultural assumptions of what mission is. We have all sat through a service that was commendably aimed at the conversion of new believers, knowing that in that congregation every single service is aimed at that outcome, and feeling unmet in our own need as established Christians mid-way through our faith journey. The Church needs to stop passing everything it does through the sieve of an arbitrary definition of 'mission'; far too much of our Christian lives are left in the sieve. While Liam Fraser's discussion of worship is not limited to its role as the foundation for mission, he leaves the corollary – that worship has other functions too – rather underdeveloped in his argument.

Another part of Christian life that is completely missed in the Five Marks, and alluded to only in passing by Fraser, is the spiritual growth and development of mature believers. The second Mark of Mission talks of the nurturing of new believers, but not of old ones. Fraser talks of individual (as well as corporate) worship, but it was perhaps not the aim of his article to develop that further. So, the second step I would take is to recover, within the Church's priorities, the deepest and most critical activity of all, which is the life-long growth of individual spirituality through personal prayer, discipleship and obedience. The experience of the numinous, the sense of being brushed by the divine, the writing of poetry on the soul, the heart-skip of a cadence of sacred music, the illumination of understanding by some 'new licht' shed by the Spirit; where is any of these in the Five Marks, or indeed in any Presbytery Mission Plan?

This is not of mere semantic interest; this imperfect, incomplete understanding of the life and work of the Church has been used as that sieve, and people's church lives are being reshaped beneath their very feet as a result.

The harm we risk

The most dramatic result of this vast omission in the legislation has been catastrophic, and it lay in the Asset

Management Buildings Audit, that Procrustean bed on which every church building in our denomination was laid in 2022. The criteria were 'well-equipped spaces in the right places', and 'well-equipped' was, so far as I can make out, interpreted as 'well-equipped for the purposes of the Five Marks of Mission and nothing else'. Buildings had to be suitable for weekday activities, community use, service of the poor, teaching of the young; and if they did not pass that utterly utilitarian test they were categorised for closure.

If the measure had included the substance of worship (corporate and individual), the numinous, the things that inspire the soul, Liam's worship, my personal holiness, then the final list of Category A buildings, the ones we get to keep, would have been rather different. A number of beautiful buildings suitable only for traditional worship might have passed that different test; a number of horrible but functional buildings could have been happily lost. Most of you will be able to name a few of each.

The Church, we often remind ourselves, is the people not the buildings. So that most dramatic and painful result of the false reliance on 'mission' (and on one arbitrary definition of mission) is not the most important result. That lies deeper, in a corporate failure to consider the most intimate parts of our spiritual lives. That must be the bottom line, surely?

How did this happen? How did we come to place so much reliance on something that was not given the length and rigour of consideration we would normally have given to a fundamental of our belief? How did we come up with a mandate for all our activities that failed to name the substance of the experience to which we try to recruit people? How have we ended up with a word, 'mission', that is weaponised by people who dismiss other people's attempts at ministry or planning because theirs are different definitions, or they belong to my brave band of mission-sceptics?

It is not the fault of those who are implementing it; the messengers should not be shot. Central staff and Presbytery office-bearers are making the best of the legislation in front of them, commendably stretching it as far as they can to meet real-life circumstances.

The catastrophe of money, buildings and personnel reached emergency proportions a few years ago, and those who were in the place to be able to see it rightly persuaded the rest of us that drastic action was necessary. Our strategists did what they could very quickly and presented a way forward to a bewildered and worried Church full of frantically busy people who did not have the time, energy or expertise to scrutinise what they were offered closely enough to find its weaknesses. They – we – took what was offered to us because doing nothing was not an option, and we did not have the capacity to come up with an alternative. That last sentence could be uttered by most members of most Presbyteries describing what was subsequently given and said to them by the people who then constructed the Presbytery-level versions of those drastic measures in their Mission Plans. It is no-one's fault; actually, we almost got it right.

It is easy with hindsight to spot the yawning gaps, the disastrous failures that led to heart-breaking decisions that were usually but not always for the best. In the implementation phase of the Church's local restructuring, beginning in many places in 2023, there is scope for some recovery. After all, the legislation requires that we take into account the Five Marks of Mission, but that does not prevent Presbyteries from taking into account the missing pieces that Liam Fraser and I have named, and the missing pieces we have not named and which the reader is astonished I have not spotted as the end of this argument approaches.

God bless the Presbytery that dares to create a space that is holy and nothing else, in some peaceful corner. God bless the

Presbytery that centres its discipling initiatives on the nearest pilgrim route. God bless the Presbytery that mandates one congregation to focus on spiritual direction, while another nearby looks after the evangelistic outreach.

Meanwhile, the Church needs to double down on the way it makes its policy and laws, the way it discerns God's will for institutions and individuals, the way it is led and directed, the way it finds the priorities it should privilege.

The lecture that follows (chapter 2A) reflects on the question of how a Church is supposed to make well the kind of decision I think we have made badly. The lectures that follow after that take a different turn, towards those questions of governance and decision-making in our Presbyterian system.

1B CONTRIBUTION FROM ANDY BRAUNSTON MINISTER FOR DIGITAL WORSHIP UNITED REFORMED CHURCH

Musings on Mission in the United Reformed Church

Who Are We?

The United Reformed Church is a union of four differing but similar traditions. Founded in 1972, that great era of Church Unions around the globe, it brought together almost all the Presbyterian Church of England and about three-quarters of the Congregational Churches of England and Wales. In 1981 about half of the Churches of Christ in Great Britain joined – this was a small restorationist movement committed to encapsulating the values of the earliest Church which they saw as shared leadership, Believer's Baptism, weekly Communion, and a search for organic unity. In the year 2000 most of the Congregational Union of Scotland joined. (Many URC folk in England see themselves as close cousins of the Kirk; many URC folk in Scotland see their heritage as one of being rather annoying to the Kirk since around 1840!) While the URC could not be seen as a takeover of any tradition by the other, our structure and order has a more Presbyterian than Congregational character.

We are, generally, socially liberal. The English Congregationalists had ordained women since 1917. We decided in the 1990s that homosexuality was no bar to membership or ordination. In 2016 we allowed ministers and churches who wished to offer marriage to same sex couples to do so whilst, at the same time, saying we have no one view on human sexuality. The URC is mixed theologically with smaller groupings of evangelicals and liberals but mainly being middle of the road. My own experience as a married gay man has been very positive in the URC. We are an increasingly "honest church" and wanting to advance an honest faith but that means we are honest about wanting a Church which both serves its members and its community. I wonder if that is a perversion of the very idea of mission. We are appropriately self-critical – most recently evidenced by our Assembly's decision to roll out compulsory anti-racist training to ministers and office holders.

We've declined dramatically over the last 50 years. The Congregational nature ethos of the URC makes it hard for Synods – our version of Presbyteries – to close a congregation against its will. This means that ministers are often spread thinly with, on average, 3 or 4 congregations each. Our demographic is certainly towards the upper range of the age spread despite an excellent Children and Youth Work department.

Justice and inclusion are at the heart of how we think though, post-Christendom, we can't really have much impact. Our ecumenical vision is strong. About a third of our congregations are Local Ecumenical Partnerships with the Methodists; we also have LEPs with Anglicans and Baptists and, in Scotland, we have five with the Kirk. This, however, may blunt whatever justice based missiological distinctives we might have.

We struggle with our own identity –we say we're committed to ecumenism but the hopes of further unions into a larger united church have been dashed. We're disappointed, and rather confused, that this hasn't happened.

Most URC folk find evangelism extraordinarily difficult. We might struggle to articulate the difference that Christ makes, we may not want to suggest that other religious traditions are lacking, and we're often very middle class and find talking about faith almost as embarrassing as talking about sex!

Understandings of Mission

Much of Marjory's first paper resonated with my experience of the URC. We've told our ministry students and such of our members who listen, that the Church doesn't have a mission but is the mission of God. After a moment's uncertainty where people wonder what on earth that means, they nod sagely and, if in college, write their essays dutifully loving David Bosch and all who follow him. *Missio Deo*, while refreshingly decentring the Church, does leave confusion because the discernment required to tease out priorities is sharpened and intensified; the potential for dispute is heightened.

We are critical of European attempts to evangelise other cultures and are comfortable at seeing this as a colonial enterprise. The London Missionary Society was founded, mainly by Congregationalists in 1795, and they sent missionaries all over the world. The LMS transformed itself between 1966 and 1977 into the *Council for World Mission*, which sees itself as a partnership of equals working together in mission; we're enthusiastic members. The CWM's understanding of mission has long been about deconstructing colonial theology and thought; it is committed to the *missio dei* paradigm.

In 1999 we adopted a major report "Growing Up", based on the Five Marks of Mission, intending to set a mission strategy for a generation. Yet very few now know this even ever existed, let alone what it might have said. In 2010 we adopted a series of vision statements meant to inform our journey over the next 10 years. Like many aspirational statements they didn't deliver what they promised; perhaps like many institutions in that era we felt that making the statement was the same as making the aspiration happen.

In our own Scottish national context the Synod has adopted, and occasionally revisits, a table of Synod Aspirations.[12] These present a picture of a church committed to inclusivity, ecological discipleship, a broad and locally-rooted menu of worship, every-member discipleship development and issues of justice and peace. For us in Scotland, these would be the lens through which any considerations of mission would be viewed. Interestingly, these do address the core issues of worship and discipleship development that is often lacking in mission statements and strategies.

The 5 Marks of Mission were at their height of popularity in the 1990s, but they've never gone away and our current thinking about them not uncritical. There is a wry humour in that no one can ever list all five of them without stumbling but there is interest in an attempt to rework them by one of our theological tutors, Graham Adams who uses ecological and liberation theology:[13]

---

[12] https://www.urcscotland.org.uk/synod-aspirations
[13] Adams, Graham, Holy Anarchy: Dismantling Domination, Embodying Community, Loving Strangeness. SCM London 2022

1. Hear the groans of creation and address the systems that exploit
2. Hear the cries of the oppressed and address the systems that exploit
3. Care for those bruised by life
4. Build communities of good news
5. Witness to the story of good news

This reworking certainly pushes many URC buttons but doesn't address Marjory's comments about worship and faith development. Perhaps the reworking of Mark 4 is wider and might include ongoing faith formation.

We have an order of ministry called *Church Related Community Workers* who have a calling to work in the community alongside the Church. They're like Church of Scotland Deacons. They would certainly see the purpose of their ministry in Mark 2. We only have 15 or so of them, however, so their valuable work is rare.

Changing the Narrative

For some years the URC has almost subconsciously been challenging the *missio dei* narrative. Daily Devotions – emailed readings, short reflections and prayers are sent to over 4,000 people each day. These bite sized chunks of a good Reformed discipline of Biblical reading and reflection have given a broad way of praying and thinking together. These are also reworked into small group discussion resources which allows people to discuss the ideas within them. We used the Devotions mailing list during Covid to send out an audio recording of worship and quickly saw how much we missed the experience of worship and how worship was key to our lives. Post Covid the URC created my role to allow me to undertake this work full time rather than alongside a four-church pastorate. We stumbled on something we should have known – we hunger for both worship and spiritual growth.[14]

Whatever else the Church does, worship is foundational to our life together. Worship gives us the energy to serve our communities, the strength to witness to our faith, the passion we need to evangelise - or at least it should! Worship matters. Not for nothing to we name our clergy "ministers of the Word and Sacraments" and expend a large part of our resources in training and sustaining them. Similarly, we give a lot of resources to train lay preachers so that the people of God are themselves nurtured and sustained in worship.

My role also includes providing a range of resources to help local churches have good worship even when they have no one trained to lead. Our _Worship Notes_[15] – rather like the Church of Scotland Starters for Sunday but with more detail – have proved transformative for struggling congregations. Congregations can even download the services as a PowerPoint file where audio and video files allow a whole service to be led remotely. Instead of people having to muddle through themselves we've found a way – imperfect and sometimes a bit clunky – at giving an experience of worship which uplifts, stimulates and inspires (in a very understated URC way of course).[16] It's too early to say if this will result in greater energy, stability and, dare I say it, "mission" in our churches but it's clear that it's helping thoughtful discipleship and spiritual enrichment.

So, for me, even before we think about mission we need to think about worship. It's the key thing that people engage with.

---

[14] See also this blog post by the Very Rev'd Kelvin Holdsworth, Provost of the Scottish Episcopal Church's St Mary's Cathedral in Glasgow https://tinyurl.com/ms442dw
[15] https://urc.org.uk/your-faith/prayer-and-worship/worship-notes/
[16] https://devotions.urc.org.uk/pulpit-supply-material/

Those seeking to find faith will come to worship, those looking to sustain and renew faith will do so through worship. Those looking to make a difference will find strength in worship. In worship we find ourselves, or should find ourselves, challenged, renewed and strengthened for service.

[The appendix that follows has no official status yet, but tries to encapsulate something of how we in the URC as part of a wider Reformed tradition value worship and how it is the heart of what we do feeding into this thing called mission.]

Worship in the United Reformed Church

Worship is vital. It is the single most important thing the Church does. In worship God makes saving love known to us; the Risen Lord draws us, through the Holy Spirit, into the presence of the Most High that we might discern God's will and purpose.[17] Through worship we are given the strength and inspiration to witness, evangelise, and serve.

Worship is grounded in Scripture. Reformed worship always places Scripture at the centre of the liturgy. Believing that with the assistance of the Holy Spirit, the Word of God is revealed in the Bible, we believe the task of the preacher is to explore that Word and bring it alive to God's people today through critical reflection, faithful exposition, contextual awareness, and sensitive preaching.[18]

---

[17] see The URC Service Book (1989) Preface by Colin Gunton p vi
[18] see the Basis of Union paras 12 & 13

Worship is both catholic and reformed.[19] We draw far and wide for liturgical patterns and words - reaching back to the earliest days of the Church, exploring across the ages, and examining the rich variety of contemporary material. Yet our tradition follows the broad pattern of the Western Church's worship with a particular emphasis on the insights of the 16th Century reformers, especially John Calvin. Calvin held the true Church was to be found wherever the Word was truly preached and heard, and the sacraments of Baptism and the Lord's Supper duly administered according to Christ's institution.[20]

Worship is liturgical. In the Reformed tradition we are mindful of St Paul's injunction that worship should be done decently and in order.[21] URC worship is always liturgical - sometimes that liturgy is known only to the leader of worship, most often it is shared in an order of service. Our predecessors' rejection of legally imposed prayer books did not mean they rejected all concepts of order. While our tradition resists any prescribed fixed liturgy - only our Baptism, marriage, and ordination services have texts which must be used – there is a sense of freedom in which our worship which allows us to respond in the moment to the promptings of the Spirit and the needs of the day. This does not mean we reject the concept of order in favour of anything goes or a free-for-all.[22]

Worship is musical. St Augustine observed that to sing is to pray twice - with our minds and our bodies. The Reformation restored congregational singing to the life of the Church, and we sing, in a variety of styles, material written in every age. Psalms and hymns embody our praise and pain, patience, and persistence.

---

[19] see the Basis of Union paras 1 - 9
[20] see The URC Service Book (1989) preface p vii
[21] see I Cor 14:40
[22] see John Huxtable's preface to the 1980 "A Book of Services"

Worship is ecumenical. Many of our congregations are local ecumenical partnerships with a range of other traditions. Our ecumenical commitments mean we've paid great attention to denominational convergence in forms of worship in recent years and have been enriched by patterns of worship which differ from our own.

Worship is always changing. Reformed Christians are aware that the Church is always in need of reformation under the Word of God; this need to be renewed and purified is also true of worship. We live with the tension of creating liturgies which seek to resonate with both our contemporaries and our traditions as language and understandings change.[23] In recent years we have been careful to use inclusive language about people and to expand our language about God with a range of Biblical images to give better expression to the truth that God is beyond all our notions of sex and gender.[24]

Worship is contextual. Leaders of worship should know and understand both their own context and that of the congregation. Preachers help the congregation gain a greater understanding of their own situation and responsibilities through skilful engagement with Scripture. Contextual worship helps us understand ourselves, the world, and God more fully that we may be better equipped for service.[25] This understanding may be enhanced through the exploration of counter-cultural ideas as we are challenged to be committed disciples and encounter the mystery that is the Triune God.

---

[23] see Worship From the URC preface by John Young para 2
[24] see GA 1984 Record of Assembly p22 requiring URC publications to use inclusive language about people and GA 2014 Record of Assembly page 24 asking that leaders of worship
[25] see Ephesians 4: 11 - 16

Worship is well resourced. As Reformed Christians we believe that we have to offer God our best in worship as well as in life. Our ministers train for several years to be competent in their various roles. Our Assembly Accredited Lay preachers train for at least two years to enjoy the Assembly's confidence that they can lead worship competently within our tradition. Increasingly Elders and others must lead worship with little or no training and the URC provides many resources to help them and all who lead worship: **Worship Notes** which, week after week, give a complete set of prayers and resources to build into a sermon for each Sunday of the year. **Politics in the Pulpit** is a weekly podcast which seeks to link contemporary events with the upcoming readings and **Talking Absolute Worship** is a recorded discussion between three or four ministers looking at the readings and what we might do with them in worship. We also provide a weekly URC service in PowerPoint format which can be downloaded ahead of time and used as a form of pulpit supply.

1C A CHURCH WITHOUT WALLS: WHAT THEY DID A GENERATION AGO
From *Speaking from the Heart*

If Burke and Churchill were right, and those who will not learn from history are condemned to repeat it, perhaps there are parts of our history so nourishing to us that we'd be condemned *if we didn't* repeat them. Perhaps there are Big Ideas we once began to put into action, but we ran out of puff because our puff was being used for more urgent and less important crises. Here is a reminder of what some of us who are now older tried when we were younger, for we hope there are people with enough puff to complete what we began.

The Special Commission: 'Church Without Walls'

The General Assembly of 1999 got into one of those fankles that the General Assembly never admits it has. The perennial debate about executive authority between Assemblies, and about the existence of the then-constantly-morphing and now-defunct Assembly Council, brought out the most contentious instincts in the leading characters of that year. There seemed to be a choice before the Assembly: to change the clothes of the Council once again, or to pause for a year or two and undertake a deeper study of questions about review and reform of the Church, a Church which always remembers the Reforming motto 'semper reformanda' (treated elsewhere in this collection).

It never ceases to amaze those who have ever served the Assembly at close quarters that such a large and cumbersome body has the ability to come to such elegant and intelligent solutions to knotty problems faced by the Church's administration. It is rare for the Assembly to achieve an outcome that seems ugly and unnecessary. The General Assembly of 1999 probably did so though, when it decided *both* to reform the existing institution a little further *and* to set up a Special Commission to look at those underlying questions. Probably it wasted thousands of hours of some people's time, and it is to be hoped they will never realise who they were. And yet, in the Special Commission itself, an amazing phenomenon produced more changes in congregational life than any other single Report of the decade.

The Commission in the course of its two years of deliberations wrestled over the curious question whether Presbyterianism could be described as institutionalised distrust, but perhaps they were tempted by that conclusion only when they were most tired. The 1999 Assembly, for all its faults, illustrated that Presbyterianism at its best is institutionalised trust, when it appointed a 'Special Commission anent Review and Reform in the Church' with its membership having an average age below 40, and its Convener being Peter Neilson.

For two years the hugely disparate group encountered each other, befriended each other, allowed themselves to be spiritually developed and encouraged by Peter, and wrestled with the most frustrating, challenging and exciting questions about the

Church's mission. Daring honesty was expressed, sacred cows were questioned, and completely different ways of living out the Church's life were explored. The more complicated the task before them became, the more the group felt the desire to bring the simplest possible Report, literally a two-word quote from Jesus: 'follow me' – with everything else the Commission needed to say contained in a large Appendix. They resisted the temptation.

The 'Church Without Walls' Report

The Special Commission brought its final report – by now known as 'Church Without Walls' – to the Assembly of 2001.[26] It has generated huge initiatives in every layer of the Church's structures, producing a generational change for the whole institution. Even those ministers and congregations who were not inclined to engage with it directly have been affected for good by its results, and most are involved with its indirect effects, some of them without realising it.

Regionally, a struggle for reform of Presbyteries was waged for fifteen years after the Report was received by the Church. The Special Commission was not the kind of body to achieve the transformation it knew was needed, and others wrestled with new ideas and old resistances. There were fiefdoms to be dismantled. There were interests invested in the crazy disparity in Presbytery sizes; when Presbyteries, unit by unit, played their constitutional part in the approval of major legislative change, two tiny Presbyteries outvoted one massive one (and on current theological spread around Scotland this gave one end of the theological spectrum a disproportionate power). A great deal of

---

26

https://www.churchofscotland.org.uk/__data/assets/pdf_file/0006/11787/CWW_REPORT_for_website_2Nov2012.pdf self-interest stood in the path of regional reform. Under the determined guidance of the last two Principal Clerks, however, the map has been redrawn. The difficult tasks are in the hands of those capable to do them, and the human assets that are the drivers of the regional Church are sensibly distributed for the first time in a long time.

Congregational life, though, was the central focus of the Commission's work. The Report confirmed the understanding of the Church that the national and regional structures exist to serve the local Church, which exists largely still in the form of congregations. Transparency was one hallmark of the changes: Kirk Sessions now meet openly, as Presbyteries had always done, and committees all over the Church publish their minutes. Simplicity is another hallmark: hundreds of congregations have escaped from the tortuous separation of apparently 'spiritual' and apparently 'temporal' decisions by transferring to the Unitary Constitution, leaving everything to the authority of the Kirk Session, and allowing the engagement of individual talents and passions in a structure of groups and appointments suited in every congregation to its exact needs and resources. The third hallmark has been celebration: gatherings, seminars, exhibitions and rallies have punctuated the Church's life ever since 2001, attracting many people's enthusiasm and leaving many others utterly uninspired and cheerfully unengaged, but that is the breadth and glory of the Church.

Without Walls?

It was a single principle, more than any structural suggestion or sequence of events, that was the genius of the Report, and represents the most difficult thing the Church can try to bring to life. 'A Church Without Walls' asked all of us to remove walls, and things like walls, in our church lives, to resist the temptation to be a community apart from community, a world separate from the world. In a Reformed Church that did not retain the tradition of enclosed monastic life, the principle demanded that the whole Church does not allow itself to be one great separate group.

The principle badly needed – and twenty years on still needs – to be broadcast. In one parish after another, the effort of ministers and people is designed to persuade local people to walk through the door of a building and attend something that is happening there for them. It may be a service or an meeting of some kind, it may be an explicitly religious event or a social activity, it may be designed to attract new people or be part of the routine of existing members; but it requires a person to come from outside into the inside, to step over a threshold – through a wall – that will not be an insignificant or invisible line to them. That is a Church defined by walls.

A dying congregation, whose membership is currently in denial and whose epitaph will be written in only a few years, proudly announces on its beautiful notice board that local people can come inside and get together for coffee and chat. The local population do nothing of the kind. They have no reason whatsoever to make the time to do so, have no idea who will be there already, do not need any more friends than they have, and would need to know what the chat was about anyway. On the local bus they pass the lovely building and are probably delighted that something so pretty sits there in the middle of their community, especially if they might want to be married there, or need it for a particularly large funeral. But why on earth would anyone open that door, walk through it, and drink coffee and chat? The people who put the notice up really thought they were doing something new and attractive; but *they* have no difficulty crossing that threshold, for *they* have been doing it for years and *they* know who else is in there with them.

By contrast, an infamously enterprising minister (and former member of the Special Commission) spotted the newly-vacated Woolworth shop in the town his parish served. Faster than it would take to think of reasons not to do it, he had a plan to take it over during Advent and make it part of the life of the town for a few weeks, benefiting the Church but rubbing out any imagined boundary-line between the congregation and the wider community. The community was involved, nowhere near the Church's own walls.

There are, of course, church walls people love to enter. The national Church has been the guardian, for good or ill, of much of the built heritage of Scotland, and thousands of people from around the world and down the road are delighted to cross the threshold and wonder at the meaning of the stones and glass. The latest process of Presbytery Planning, with its Asset Management Buildings Audit already mentioned (well done not to invent a more theological-sounding phrase, which would have added insult to the injury) is our way of admitting we can no longer afford to prioritise such guardianship, which is why it is so sad for so many in so many places.

And yet, in a distinctively Scottish way, our denomination is translating into its own practices the best of the 'cathedral tradition' in England, the phenomenon by which church growth bucks the more general trend of decline in the great historic places of ceremonial, expert musicianship, ancient art and continuity of familiar worship. The point is that people come to those spaces because they are the very special spaces they are, not because they are our spaces where we invite, require, chivvy people to come onto our territory. Too often the majesty of our church space is removed and replaced with bits of paper, notice-boards, electronic displays, TV screens, all proudly narrating the churchy busy-ness of people who behave as if they own the place. They stomp all over the magic of the atmosphere, and take away its peace, the relief its quietness will bring to noisy souls who might be fortunate enough to find it just when they need it. So the Church, even where it has the most beautiful buildings, has to be a Church without walls by letting anyone permeate those walls, coming in and going out, without pressure and – please God – without clutter.

And people permeate our walls, in their thousands, at Watchnight. They come for reasons it would be impertinent and condescending to analyse. Those reasons may have to do with memories of something that was taught to people, held as precious and never entirely lost, something they need to touch on that magic day. Those reasons probably include the things that are happening on that occasion: resonant music, familiar words, the anonymity of darkness and a crowd, the luminal mystery of the midnight hour. Those reasons, surely, *surely*, have absolutely nothing to do with the regular congregation inviting the others to come and join them in their space on that day at that hour. The Church need only make the slightest intimation that the service is taking place – or in most places just do nothing to suggest that it won't – and the people materialise with very clear expectations, in numbers so large that they have the confidence to do something they would not do alone. The normal Sunday attendees are hardly the reason anyone came.

That is a bonus, to have people permeating the walls from outside. The real question is whether the members of congregations really succeed in breeching the walls from within, to reach the world with the doing of good things and the telling of good words and the manifesting of good promises. Yet another

Special Commission[27] (you can tell something niggles the Church if several Commissions address similar questions in close succession) examined the national Church's responsibility to provide the ordinances of religion to Scotland as a whole. Overwhelmingly it discovered that Scottish institutions, significant individual leaders, and those in the very machinery of public service, still expected the Church of Scotland to provide its distinctive ministry throughout the communities of this country. Scotland may be more diverse than secular; or if she is secular she somehow does not deny a spiritual need.

Inner Walls

That, however, is largely about physical spaces. The Church, with or without its defining walls, is the place where I and millions like me confess a most terrifying truth; that though my body is filled with physical stuff, bones, muscles, organs, blood – filled right up tight so no spaces would be found if an anatomist were to cut me open – yet when I look in to myself I feel as if there is space there, huge space in which my mind moves about and my fears shiver and my passions pull me about, space enough to meet other people and to meet God whatever God may look like. That space, invisible and almost indescribable, is the most sacred of all. The Church has permission to occupy it, and must do so with an infinitely tender sensitivity. The Church has the responsibility to talk about it, and must do so with the most carefully-chosen words. It is what in the National Youth Assembly sometimes was called 'the middle of your middle', and it is a fearful thing to become aware of it. This too suffers from the building of walls, the keeping out or keeping in of the spirit, the posing of boundaries that should not be there.

---

[27] Special Commission on the Third Article Declaratory, see Volume of General Assembly Reports, Edinburgh: Assembly Arrangements Committee 2010.

Entrance exams of many kinds are used to establish who is inside an artificial spiritual boundary and who remains an outsider. At one theological end of the Church especially, bald propositions of personal *faith* are posed for assent, rejecting any possibility that people find the claims of the Gospel complex, intriguing, mysterious. There is expected of them a brutal 'yes', as if to a closed question of some kind, but with that assent they are welcomed as if they have made in an instant the whole length of the journey from evil to good, from reprobate to saved, from beyond to within. Their personal spiritual space belongs safely inside a clearly defined wall. In all sorts of parts of the Church particular habits of *worship* are demanded as an irreducible norm, as if the artistic tastes of those who maintain those patterns are an archetype given by God. Those who can manage to love those practices (and they may be anything from mass settings to praise bands, from silence to Victorian organ-music) are regarded as acceptable, and there is no moral duty to try to make sense for other people whose ears are just differently wired. The dominant group have an aesthetic sense that secures them within a wall of their own arbitrary taste. In yet another part of the Church an intellectual preacher is mismatched to a parish that has the temerity to be full of not especially intellectual people, and casts around it a barrier of *language* that excludes most of the population. The minister, obviously, has not grasped the difference between intelligent preaching and intellectual preaching, and enjoys the latter far too much. A small coterie adores the stimulus; while the great majority discover that there is too great a distance to drive conveniently on a snowy Sunday morning to hear the neighbouring minister talk plain English. The space around which a wall is keeping them out is a mental space, and no-one should have the right to keep them out as if from a beautiful garden.

That is all extremely comfortable for the individuals who step within the boundaries that are put in front of them, who decide to enter the magic circle that is offered to them. The vast majority who do not are left untouched by the Church, as if they deserved to be ignored now for not being attracted by the narrow offering extended to them in the first place. The real wickedness of it lies in the laziness of those who place those invisible walls where they find them easiest to maintain for themselves: laziness because they are not breaking down the walls, moving across those boundaries and bringing love, care and service to those waiting outside.

There are, happily, too many people who give the lie to that lazy, exclusive way. There are just too many lovely people who make the world a better place but who do not have a sense of belonging securely and confidently in some part of the spectrum of the Church. There are just too many people who barely make it through the threshold of the Church, who sit – figuratively or literally – close to the door for an easy escape, and who patently live loving, sacrificial, outward-facing lives beyond the Church door. The shy beadle, who does far more than she is paid to do but does not believe that she could possibly become a member of an important organisation like the Church, because it is for better than the likes of her, is acting heroically every time she steps inside her workplace. The single parent bringing her child to the after-school club and loving it, but lacking the courage to come to Church at the weekend and sit alone without the excuse of her child to strengthen her, is troubled by the walls. The frail old gentleman who relishes the Afternoon Club in the Church hall once a week, where not only will he have tea and cakes but also a wee sing of a Moody and Sankey hymn remembered from his youth, has found the Church comes through its own walls to the place where he manages to be comfortable.

Chaplains Without Walls

In one large area of the Church's ministry, working without and outwith walls has always been normal. Chaplaincies are spreading through more and more of society's institutions, defying the secularising narrative and creating touching-points between the Gospel and everyday life. In hospitals, prisons, the Armed Forces, industry, commerce and every kind of place of education, chaplains find themselves cast into someone else's world with the challenge of making it as naturally their own world as if they were in a comfortable familiar building, the kind with funny glass and strange furniture. They are thrown into situations full of people the Church would not otherwise meet or serve, and they have to live on their wits, bereft of the equipment and sacred space most parish ministers take for granted.

The institutional Church feels nervous sometimes, because modern employment law has forced a shift for chaplains, away from the total control of their religious institution and into the secular employment of the place where they serve. NHS chaplains employed by the local trust, prison chaplains employed by the Scottish Prison Service; these and others lack another wall, a wall of institutional protection around them, keeping them to the tasks their Churches would like them to be doing, and exposed instead to their new world and its demands. They have to be trusted massively by the denominations that have sent them, trusted to keep faith with the fundamentals of their calling, trusted to exercise a recognisable ministry far beyond all sorts of ecclesiastical walls. The trust too comes from the receiving institution, the school or hospice or military establishment or oil company; these places welcome chaplains who have been sent their way with such freedom and responsibility.

There are, of course, other tempting walls to be found when they have arrived. The chaplain is quickly gathered into the walls of the institution in which she is meant to minister, learning its codes, following its routines, obeying its timetables, implementing its protocols, finding her place in its structures of authority and leadership. She discovers all over again the same dynamics of personal interaction, political intrigue, and good and evil, that she knew when she was sheltered inside the Church. She may be tempted to remain within these new walls, literal ones that hide her in a small space marked 'Chaplaincy', or the more important ones inside her head, that limit what she believes she can do and who she believes really needs her time and attention. Perhaps she will be the person who breaks down the needless walls of her new environment and does it a service it did not expect from her. Perhaps her own invisible walls of self-doubt and limited vision will be destroyed by the new possibilities she sees, to do things she has never seen the Church able to do before.

Bursting Walls

From time to time in the Church's history, some bursting out of energy has marked a terrifying and uncertain time, a time on which we look back with gratitude and a sense of the world transformed. The first Apostles, breaking out of their lives to set fire to the whole known world; the adventurer saints in the Middle Ages, taking possession of whole new countries in Northern Europe for the cause of Christ; the orders of friars, bringing fresh life to the preaching of the Gospel for ordinary people; the Reformers, Protestant and Catholic, re-connecting the Church with the biggest claims of the Gospel: every one of those movements broke down boundaries and barriers, limits and limitations. World-changers in those eras invaded society around them and took away the excuse people had – *the excuse we too often still give them by hiding from them* – for ignoring what the Church is about and what the Church has to say.

Today, as we hardly dare to count the number of people who say they belong within our walls, we have learned – perhaps in the nick of time – that this is a foolish number to rely on. The elusive measure of our social capital should matter more to us, though it hardly suits journalists and critics who like a finite membership statistic – and ideally a plummeting one. Too often Churches draw an imaginary ring around particular articles of faith and then count the people who are able to assent to those articles, who feel they are standing within that ring. Aren't we, rather, called to realise that there are far more people who stand further out from the centre of our beliefs, gladly within earshot of the Gospel and earnestly living with all the integrity and purity they can manage? Today, as church buildings all over the country are refurbished as those 'well-equipped spaces in the right places'[28] to make them more like other places where people feel comfortable, we are dimly grasping that there are many ways, old and new, to serve people's lives and make the whole world a wholesome, holy place.

And so the Church has embarked on its latest exercise of reconstruction or retrenchment or consolidation, the one authorised in 2021, the one with the Five Marks of Mission and the AMBA scythe. There are few things new under the sun, but in this latest round I see two lines crossed for the first time. One is the letting go of any pretence that we have a moral responsibility to maintain buildings with architectural merit that cannot be easily used for week-day activities beyond formal worship; and it is impossible to overstate the sadness that causes

---

[28]

https://www.churchofscotland.org.uk/__data/assets/pdf_file/0017/58400/General_Trustees_-_Well_equipped_spaces_in_the_right_places.pdf p10ff us all. The other is the admission that our stipendiary ministry will never be much bigger than it is now, and our parish structure might as well be carved up to match the harsh arithmetical reality (which, in any case, is all we can afford in money terms too now). That requires ministers either to change their method of ministering quite brutally, or to burst in the attempt to do everything the old way to (on average) 50% more territory and population.[29]

In doing all that, the Church has not explicitly committed to the principles of 'A Church Without Walls', but by using the language of 'mission' explored in the previous essay it has said much the same thing in different words, and it has continued in the philosophy articulated so passionately twenty years to the week before the latest planning legislation fell upon us.

---

[29] 1000 ministries are becoming 660 in the first five-year exercise. And when I say 'burst' I'm talking about mental health. Personally, my strategy has been to drop to 75% of stipend and a proportionately lighter ministerial load; I suspect it gives me both a standard of living and a job that are comparable to the ministry of my grandfather (see next chapter) in the 1940s. I believe it will preserve my sanity, but I am conscious that many ministers cannot afford to pull the same stunt.

2A CORPORATE DISCERNMENT

If it will not do to build the edifice of the Church's purpose on the pretence that mission is a self-evident thing that looks the same to all of us, how are we to determine what we should be doing? If the mission 'of' God is difficult to identify beyond those actions we humans cannot emulate (sending the Son, the Spirit), how are we to discover what our own mission is in this time and this place?

This lecture takes a look at the experience of our presbyterian-governed Church trying to discern the will of God and what that means for our vocation together to fulfil that will. This series began with a dismantling of a too-easy, vulnerable assumption that we know what it is we are supposed to be doing. Later will come discussions of how authority works in the church and how structure helps us in doing whatever the right thing is. For now, the question is how we go about discerning that 'right' thing that I've argued is not as obvious as many people think.

How, in short, does the mind of God become the mind of the Church? You know what; never mind 'how', but does it?

Prayer

If this were a lecture about individual discernment, I suppose it would be largely a reflection on the practice of personal prayer, the pursuit of revelation, vision and realisation of the path to take and the work to do. That strand of supplicatory prayer, the 'show me what you want' demand we all make in our best but most impatient moments, is sometimes triggered by circumstances we want to react to well, and sometimes triggered by a more proactive desire to be led to something new we would not have thought of all by ourselves.

Is corporate discernment a negotiation of individual discernments; the people who make up a Court or a Committee each have their own prayer-generated vision, and by discussion, mediation, or arbitration by some recognised authority a single vision emerges that becomes the institution's discerned vocation?

That would be attractive, but I fear no-one reading this believes that is what happens within our structures of governance. I leave it to you to reflect on the likely extent of the practice of personal prayer by those they encounter in our decision-making bodies. But even supposing universal diligence in spiritual practice, all too often we realise that many people in a meeting have not read the papers in advance, or pieces of business are brought without notice. We know for a certainty that we are not a gathering of individuals who have sought God's mind already on each of the things we have to address.

Then there is the human tendency to spiritual modesty that easily defers to the charismatic figure in the room, to that big-personality Convener who has thought about the issue a great deal – perhaps that is why it is on the agenda in the first place – and has a well-argued case for a particular proposal. Especially in the absence of an alternative suggestion, it is difficult to resist an idea couched in personal piety.

And this is despite the fact that certainty of vision is no guarantee of its authenticity. You only need to have served on a

Nominating Committee that has interviewed two candidates who each used the language of utter certainty of their calling to this parish, and you know how hard it is to find the words to convey 'sorry, but God didn't say that to us'.

The other thing about vision is that it is not a good candidate for compromise, which is what can too easily happen when conflicting convictions have to be combined. If Member A of the Africa Committee is convinced that its budget should be spent in Malawi, while Member B is equally sure that God is calling us to support Mozambique, the Committee may try to serve both visions by splitting the fund between the two, but fail to achieve anything really worthwhile in either place. It takes as much spiritual courage to say 'no' to a sincerely held vision as it probably took for its proponent to articulate the vision in the first place.

Corporate discernment needs to be similar to individual discernment; it needs also to involve that element of prayer.

Now don't get me started on the prayers I have heard in meetings. I have commented elsewhere on the abuse of process by the Convener whose prayer of constitution at the beginning of the meeting is a mirror to the content of the minute they hope will emerge at the end, pretending to seek illumination for the business at hand while hinting at their preferred outcome.

But what if, in every meeting of a Court or committee in the Church, a period of silent prayer was scheduled in after all the matters had been discussed and before the decisions were made? Sitting together ('together' can include presence on video-calls as long as it is genuinely attentive), members would hold the question, wait for guidance, and form – perhaps re-form – their personal view. No doubt there would still be split votes afterwards; I think I believe that would not happen very often.

I also think I believe that the Church would sometimes discover callings that had not always been in the mind of any individual before the corporate discussion began. In the course of the most thrilling of debates in the General Assembly, an idea can emerge in our midst that had been in no-one's mind at the beginning of the afternoon, a solution to a problem we thought had us stuck, a new initiative that increases our heartrates with excitement. When I conduct Session or committee meetings, my practice is to ask at the beginning of the meeting whether there is any 'other' business not on the agenda that cannot be left to a future meeting (which it should be if possible to allow for that process of prayer in advance, if you have agreed with me so far); but at the end of the meeting I always ask the question again, in case a new idea has emerged in the course of our discussions and needs to be aired.

The Necessary and the Desirable

If the conduit for vision must be prayer both individual and collective, we need criteria to test these ideas, filters to decide what is genuinely of the Spirit and what is a fanciful human dream.

One area of the Church's work has used a neat assessment process I think could be adopted much more widely. Anyone who has had responsibility for a building in the Church of Scotland in the last few decades will instantly recognise the classification of repairs as 'Urgent, Essential or Desirable'. [30] If I remember correctly, Urgent repairs were supposed to occur within one year, Essential ones within about five, and the Desirable items were tackled by congregations with the means, the workforce... and the vision. Essential items required a reaction to the state things had reached, while Desirable ones assumed a more proactive attitude. As for the Urgent – well, let me come back to that.

Imagine what would happen if we ran all our decisions – about money, outreach, community service, buildings closures,

---

[30] These terms, derived in this particular way, are capitalised throughout this discussion.

prophetic proclamation – through that 'UED' filter, and then paused to pray.

The Church frequently comes across situations in which it is simply not an option to do nothing, and a way forward has to be found. It is Essential. A deeply contentious social or political debate rages in Scottish society and it would be a dereliction of duty for the Church not to make the voice of Christian compassion heard in a time of moral uncertainty or international conflict. A disaster within the Church, perhaps the loss to fire of a significant place of worship, requires big decisions, major expenditure, allocation of human resources from one place to another. These are the decisions that are Essential, and perhaps in these the discernment of God's will is easy because the next steps are obvious to everyone.

The Church frequently, though, comes across Desirable opportunities in which there is an option to do nothing, but doing nothing might not be the wisest course nor make the best of the possibilities for Christian witness. The example earlier, of competing needs in different countries might prompt an imaginative and courageous re-allocation of effort that produces far better outcomes in the new place than were being achieved in the old, albeit requiring a hard decision that could easily have been dodged for the sake of a quiet life.

Here is an example of both, from personal recent experience. In 2021-22 I had the job of drafting the Presbytery Mission Plan for Orkney Presbytery. For those reading this far into the future, that means I was writing a text that described the 'missional' starting point of our area (I know, hard to imagine a worse candidate really, given all I've already said) and proposing in general terms the allocation of human and buildings assets in service of those Five Marks of Mission. There were lots and lots of circumstances to take into account, constraining the possibilities for our vision for the future; in Orkney many of those constraints are geographical as we try to witness in many self-contained small communities on separate land masses. There were also lots of ideas for how we would do things, and I won't list them here.

I sincerely believe, though, that we remembered both what was 'Essential' and what was 'Desirable' in expressing what we believed we were called to be and do.

The biggest Essential we had to achieve was, of course, the stretching of the assets we were permitted across the geographical challenge that faced us. The Church nationally had taken the transformative step of deciding at last to align the number of 'ministries' to the number of predicted professional posts (ministers, deacons, other paid and non-stipeniary staff) it could sustain. Nationally it would, in time, reduce the number of vacant posts from a predicted 30-40% of all ministries down to about 10% of the new number, the latter being a natural rate in a system where the time taken to fill vacancies is deemed on average to occupy 10% of the time of each congregation.

Locally in Orkney, we saw the effect of that dramatically; the Presbytery had been struggling along with a vacancy rate around 50% for years, and some congregations in very long-term vacancies had lost hope of having a conventional ministry again. Our new allocation of staffing was higher than the number of staff we actually had in post at the point the planning process began; so, unlike many Presbyteries, our problem was not to reduce our numbers overall but to re-allocate those assets so that the vacancies would dissolve in a new and different way of ministering.

We borrowed an idea already implemented in Shetland, and produced a Plan for a pan-Orkney Team Ministry with a (notional, technical) union of congregations and Kirk Sessions into one. Two strategies were agreed that would liberate enough of each minister's time to take on pastoral responsibility for more than their current charge: one was that losing of local Kirk Sessions to moderate and lead; the other was the re-structuring of some tasks to be carried out across the whole county (one person doing all the GDPR, one person doing all the youth development, and so on).

Some people hate it, both ministers and Kirk Sessions. But it was the way the majority chose to fulfil the Essential task that was the purpose of the new legislation. We could minister realistically to the whole of Orkney, for the first time in a long time.

The pan-Orkney aspect of our ministries, and the substantial pastoral ministries that are replacing old interim moderatorships; these challenge us to minister as effectively in the places where ministers are not resident as in the places where we live. As I wrote this, before the Union is brought into effect, larger congregations are getting their heads round 'their' ministers spending time in smaller places, are learning to love live-streamed services connecting together some unlikely new partners, and are realising that by the wonders of Zoom it often doesn't matter whether your minister is 100 feet away or at the other end of a weather-affected ferry trip.

In doing all this, though, we hoped to achieve some other, Desirable, benefits. Those long-term vacancies did not just lack an inducted ministry; some of them were so small that they had insufficient leadership to ensure frequency of worship or any weekday church activities or attraction of new members or replenishment of eldership. It was difficult to point to signs of church life and presence in some places, where individual Christians were living faithful lives but were doing so without the benefit of the structures that a previous generation would expect the national Church to provide in their local situation.

Our Plan talks of ministry within the burgeoning renewable energy sector, the sharing of the best practice in youth ministry between the island where it is strongest and the parishes where it is non-existent, the upscaling of outreach through the county's pilgrim trails. These things are not to be found directly in the legislation that required the planning to be done, but the idea of them brings a smile.

So much for the Essential and Desirable; that leaves the tyranny of the Urgent.

How often would you characterise a bad or needless decision like this: 'Something needed to be done; this was something, so we did it'?

In the best-intentioned of imperfect, fallen, human ways, we rush into things we think are no-brainers. We do it in two ways.

First, sometimes our Courts and Committees are so spooked by the urgency of a situation that they do not consider whether it is either Essential or Desirable to do what they assume they have to get on and do. A classic example of this in recent times has been the presumption of every congregation upon becoming vacant that there is only one thing to do, to recruit a new minister as soon as possible. The complete re-wiring of all our heads by the Presbytery Mission Plan Act, the eradication of all presumptions about where ministry should be located, the re-founding of ministry on the mission foundation previously discussed; these deny that long-held instinct to replenish the previous pattern of ministry whenever a gap appears.

When this happens, the mistake has been to miss out the crucial step of discernment, to fail to realise there is a decision of principle to be made before the administrative process is begun.

Second, sometimes the problem is not with the necessity of action, but there is simply an excess of haste that prevents the best tactic being followed. Alongside this lecture is 'Filling a Vacancy' from the *Speaking from the Heart* collection. There I invite you to consider how often a Nominating Committee draws too restrictively the range of ministerial types it is willing to consider suitable for its congregation. Sometimes, perhaps, prayerful discernment is needed about how to do a thing, not just whether it's a thing that needs to be done at all.

There's an intriguing twist that might be given to our Urgent-Essential-Desirable classification. Applied to fabric issues, the ones that are Urgent are invariably also Essential; they are the subset of Essential repairs that are also most time-critical. I'd like to suggest that when it comes to the things we feel called to do as individuals or organisations, there are things that are Desirable but also Urgent. These are the things that perhaps have not been thought of much, but the opportunity to do them is right now if they are ever to be done.

We have never had a chaplaincy in that industrial unit over there, but a church-going manager has arrived and is just at the never-to-be-repeated point of allocating resources to the pastoral care of their workers. We should seize the day, make the pitch, grasp the opportunity. And if that means someone's pet project has to wind up to release their time for this, well...

To do that right every time, the same process of prayer and discernment is necessary, but might need to be accelerated to meet the moment. No-one has ever taught me to pray quickly; if anything the older I get the more slowly I try to do it. There must be moments when the Church has to pray, envision, seek revelation as quickly as she makes strategic and tactical decisions.

Too often, those are the moments in which the people who should be making the reflective decisions are too busy. They are fire-fighting whatever the emergency is, giving pastoral care to people suffering in the middle of the situation, providing instant leadership. So what they do is gladly dump the situation on the experts the Church has ready to do difficult stuff. And most of the time those experts are not our policy makers; they are our implementers. The earlier aphorism becomes 'Something must be done; we have a technical expert who knows how to do something that looks as if it would address the situation; therefore that's what we will do'.

Perhaps a congregation has been tumbled into vacancy in the most tragic circumstances, through the unexpected death of the minister. An Interim Moderator is appointed, and it is all she can do to comfort the stricken community and figure out what were the unavoidable items in the minister's diary that still need to be seen to. That mistaken decision, to move as fast as possible to permission to call a new minister, might very well be the result of the vacancy question being bounced too quickly onto the desks of the Vacancy Procedure Committee members, who go straight to the 'how' question and not the 'whether'. In the grand scheme of things, even though it's insensitive to say it at this appallingly sad time, should this congregation actually be getting permission to call at all? If on proper reflection they should indeed be given that permission, but given the circumstances that have produced the vacancy, don't they need a period of grieving before they push on to elect a Nominating Committee? All sorts of good questions like these will be asked by any of our wise and experienced Presbytery Clerks; but shouldn't they be asked by the very process itself?

When do we need to look for the moment that requires a pause for a policy decision, and when is it right to get on with the job in hand?

Policy and Administration

One of the nettles our Church needs to grasp is the development of spiritual leadership that is willing and able to make decisions of policy, not just to take the administrative steps to implement policy made somewhere else (or nowhere at all).

It is difficult enough at General Assembly level. In the Church Offices (mainly but not exclusively at 121 George Street, Edinburgh, so collectively if inaccurately referred to as '121') are located the executive and administrative staff tasked with implementing the policies made by the General Assembly and carrying out the functions common to all organisations (civil law compliance, human resources, IT support and so on). Wherever their tasks are premised on policy decisions, they report to a Committee of some sort. The committee's tricky roles are to ensure the implementation of policy that has been made by the Assembly, propose new policies to the Assembly for consideration, and make unavoidable interim policy decisions in those situations that require quick reaction.

For instance, a committee tasked with the Church's overseas work may implement an Assembly decision to develop a new resource for a partner denomination. Meanwhile, looking at another country, the committee may bring a motion to the General Assembly meeting in a few weeks' time, to condemn human rights violations of a particular type in that place, and give weight to the political voices calling out bad governance that might otherwise go unnoticed from this distance. If the crisis that calls for comment erupts soon after our Assembly has met in May, the committee will have to decide whether to make a statement straight away, sincerely assessing whether the position is aligned with the Assembly's usual approach.

So, you have voting members of the committees whose non-executive task is (small p) political, policy-making. And then you have staff members in 121 with the executive non-political task. The problem is keeping each person on their side of the dividing line, which is particularly hard for staff members who, by virtue of being ministers, deacons or elders in their own right, have a policy-making role elsewhere in the Church that tempts them to have opinions it's not strictly speaking their job to have. All of this is true in the larger Presbyteries (and everyone is currently moving into membership of these if they were not already in one of the historically big ones), because they too have paid executive staff.

If that makes it a little difficult at Assembly/121/mega-Presbytery level, there is a much more worrying problem at the level of Kirk Sessions, and the older small Presbyteries, where the people who have to make the policy are the very people who then implement it, because there is no luxury of paid staffing. Perhaps very occasionally there is a problem with policy makers inventing grand schemes and leaving others to do the donkey work (for instance where a Kirk Session gets carried away with a vision but assumes the minister will carry it out because after all that's what the stipend is for).

Far more common and destructive to the life of the Church is the opposite problem, the humility of leaders who would far prefer to be given a manageable task than to produce new ideas and visions. Try to recruit elders and you will be met with a wall of spiritual modesty, and it's too easy to negotiate the wall by assuring the person that all you are asking is a bit of practical help with fabric or fund-raising. Gradually the Kirk Session becomes more and more an efficient operational machine, less and less a locus of vision, imagination... and discernment of God's will for the Church in that place. The congregation then becomes another community enterprise, good at preserving fabric or holding fund-raising coffee-mornings but saying nothing distinctive to a community full of people who need to hear revolutionary, transformational, challenging, comforting promises that are out of this world.

Grandpa

I was born a few years after my paternal grandfather died and have always wondered what Rev John MacLean would think if he knew that the only one of his grandchildren to become a minister was a girl. His death occurred just after the generally-accepted high-point of 20th Century church life in Scotland, the original Tell Scotland crusade of the mid-50s, and his active ministry in two modest parishes (Renton, then Liff) spanned both World Wars and the inter-war years.

Of course, he was much busier with weddings and baptisms than we are now, since almost everyone wanted those from their parish churches; and he would have done all the local funerals too, something I did at the beginning of my parish ministry thirty years ago but not now.

A couple of years before he retired, a new member of the manse household arrived, when my parents married and my mother found herself looking after a large house and the two men living in it. A lifetime later, she recalled to me the rhythm of his ministry, contrasting it with mine. He would invariably have the whole morning in his study, writing correspondence, preparing the single act of worship he would be conducting that week, thinking through the papers for his committee work (he was a doyen of the Foreign Mission committees of the Church, and an arch-schemer in the Presbytery of Dundee, apparently). In the afternoons he would walk or drive out to do a bit of visiting most days. The evenings, apart from the occasional Presbytery meeting in town, would be spent enjoying the company of his baby grandson - my brother, or reading, or spending ages on the phone with his fellow-schemers late into the night.

Mother said the dynamic of parish life had changed between end of his ministry and what she saw of the early years of mine. Few people had phones back in his day, so the doorbell of the manse would be constantly ringing. By the time she was visiting me in my first charge, the doorbell was largely untroubled, but the phone would ring a dozen times a day from all corners of the parish area and beyond. And if she were still alive and visiting me now more than thirty years later, she would find the house silent most of the time apart from the click of the computer keyboard and the occasional ping of the text messages by which I largely run things now.

The point is that John MacLean didn't have GDPR, Safeguarding, Health and Safety and all the rest to clog up his ministry. Those are necessary and good things, but they don't half take up energy, even with good lieutenants to look after the forms. Grandpa had much more time to think of the big questions and to pray about the day-to-day life of his parish (that would be just the one parish, obviously, remember those?).

Just occasionally, as solitary people tend to do, I have an imaginary conversation with Grandpa as I'm driving to an engagement, and I try to explain to him what is happening. It's a challenge to describe the live-streaming of a service from one island congregation to another, or the speed of correspondence conducted invariably by e-mail and no longer glacially by post. It's mildly embarrassing to confess just how diffident one has to be in a school chaplaincy setting these days to avoid accusations of proselytisation. I think he'd be taken aback by the length of a typical Kirk Session agenda. I don't know whether he could keep up with the diaries of my full-time colleagues even in small places, and the range of non-church third sector bodies doing things the Church used to do as a matter of course might dismay him rather.

Grandpa had time. He also had two other things many ministers do not have today.

First, he had a knowledge of the Church that was genetic, being born and brought up in an active Church of Scotland household, with the language of our ways and our governance second nature to him. I am one of a diminishing cohort of contemporary ministers who can say the same; my bone marrow is presbyterian blue. But more and more of our ministers and elders come from unchurched upbringings, or from beyond the Church of Scotland or beyond Scotland itself. John's instinctive understanding of the culture of the Church, shared with all his colleagues, gave all of them a foundation of knowledge and historic wisdom that must have grounded their discernment and decisions.

Second, he had clout. Along with the dominie and the doctor, the minister was one of the few educated leaders of any community, universally recognised as such. Again, I count myself unusual in that I minister now in the kind of community, that still exists around the edges (literally) of Scotland, where the Church is noticed and people have expectations of it. In most places, the Church can only be effective by punching above the weight of its numbers, its assets, its political voice. People probably knew what John MacLean thought, and thought it mattered.

I think we have let go of our regret that his time has gone, or at least we should teach our congregations not to plan mission for the generation before last. What then, should we do instead?

Let's do less

In my time, I have rejoiced when I read that the Church of Scotland had the biggest non-statutory social work presence in the country, or the greatest social capital of any organisation in the charitable sector. I have applauded outgoing Moderators whose reports talked of our denomination punching above its weight. I have assumed that each of my parish ministries should be measured by an increase in community engagement and perhaps a greater footfall in our buildings.

In my dotage I am not so sure. I think we need, corporately as well as individually, to shut up and listen. We need to shut up and listen as part of our method of doing what we do. We need to shut up and listen instead of doing some of the things we do; because if we did shut up and listen, we might hear that those were not the things God wanted us to do because they did not in fact serve/build/usher in the Kingdom that is promised. And if we did stop doing them, then we would have liberated the time it takes to do the listening, and we'd have achieved the virtuous circle we lack.

Isn't it time to learn to punch *below* our weight?

I long for a Church that is not frantic, does not damage the mental health of those who try to keep it all going, is not running from task to task. I look for a Church in which people have time to wait, to breathe, to ask, to listen, to tell stories and make each other laugh or cry, to come slowly to a realisation of what is Desirable because – surprise! – it is desired by God. I am reconciled – more than reconciled actually – to our being a small denomination in which just 1% of the population of the country behaves in extraordinary ways in the service of astonishing promises and all because they shut up and listen.

The problem is that everyone thinks that their little bit of vision is the little bit of vision that should clearly be retained when the slimming down takes place. The convener of every working group, the elders of every worshipping community, the paid staff of every social enterprise owned by the Church, the volunteer in every friendship group believes their thing is that 'right thing' that was so elusive at the beginning of this lecture.

We have come full circle in this discussion, back to the need for mature, praying discernment by the Church performing its role as a creature quite unlike any other. We need, in a way we do not currently have, the capacity to do that properly. That requires time, courage, confidence, and the attitude (the one the world now thinks is bonkers) that the answers are not to be found in ourselves.

2B CONTRIBUTION FROM SCOTT RENNIE
MINISTER, CROWN COURT, LONDON

How can we tell? Discerning our calling together

The call to ministry is central to the vocation of any Minister of Word and Sacrament. Indeed, when one seeks the church's confirmation of one's call, it's the ability to articulate clearly that sense of call (as well as one's suitability in other ways of course) that determines whether or not that call is recognised by the church, and one goes forward for education and training for the Ministry.

One of the privileges I have had as a facilitator of Ministry Development Conversations with fellow ministers is to hear people relay to me that sense of call and its first stirrings, now some years in the past, but still present and seeking some kind of response in the here and now.

I believe in the Ministry of Word and Sacrament and have not lost faith in its centrality for the future life of the church, alongside other roles and function which makes up the ministry of the church in its widest sense. When I was asked some years ago now, if I would be prepared to undergo training in order to facilitate conversations with colleagues trying to discern 'Where now?', in their calling I was delighted to accept.

I not only have a passion for Ministry of Word and Sacrament but over these years of working alongside many colleagues, I have become passionate about the welfare of Ministers themselves, their overall happiness, and their sense of fulfilment in the task of ministry.

I think I have also learned over 23 years in ministry the reality of how lonely a role it can be, how vulnerable one can feel in ministry amidst all the pushes and pulls of expectations and calls on one's time and energy. And all this in an environment where everyone is made anxious by the increasing secularisation of society and the apparent shrinking of the institution.

The reality is that for many of us Presbytery has not always offered the collegiality we might have hoped for or felt like the place where we could openly talk about our questions in relation to our role or our context for ministry. It has not proved the place where we can continue to wrestle with the outworking of our vocation – its joys and frustrations – or about our vulnerabilities and questions as we seek to respond to the continuing call of God on our lives amidst the messiness of our ministerial context.

Ministry Development Conversations are, I believe, a gift that Ministers can give to themselves, and ought to give themselves, on their pilgrimage of faith and ministry.

These conversations create a safe and supportive space to open up, confidentially and honestly, about where one is in one's ministry, and whether or not there is a change of call apparent, or whether the means of ministry in one's context needs further discernment. They offer a space where the competing interests of personal, emotional, and spiritual wellbeing can be given voice, alongside the external pressures of family life and local and societal context.

The conversation is also an opportunity to honestly review whether the church and oneself needs to make some kind of further investment in continuing professional development to help one navigate the challenges and opportunities presenting themselves at any one time.

Ministry Development Conversations, or MDC's as we'll call them for brevity's sake, are best when approached out of curiosity. That is to say, entered into with an open spirit and not imposed as a hoop one must jump through as a means of obtaining something else from the institutional church. They are always Minister led, that is, it is the Minister's own questions about their role, their ministry, and their future that begins and informs the whole conversation between Minister and trained facilitator.

Rather like a therapist, it is not the facilitator's role to influence or impose their own thoughts and opinions, but rather to listen, question perhaps, and then reflect back to the participating Minister what they have heard.

The Conversations should be prepared for, and a rubric is offered, but in my experience as a facilitator, Ministers, by the time of the conversation, have often formulated the questions of discernment they are wrestling with by the time the conversation takes place, and it is the privilege of the facilitator to accompany them as they wrestle with these questions with a friendly and supportive ear to hand.

The rubric itself is based around these three areas for review: My role, my ministry, and my future.

Questions around 'My Role', centre on curiosity about the global sense of call and one's own wellbeing in it. Where does continuing sense of call fit with one's current practice of ministry? Are we feeling fulfilled?

Do we know what expectations are placed on us, or by ourselves, and are these proving realistic? How has our recent experience of ministry impacted on our sense of call where we are? Do we have a good work/life balance? Have there been changes in my life that have changed how I think about my calling to ministry?

Questions around 'My Ministry' focus more on one's particular context. For example, are we forming constructive and healthy relationships with our Session and office bearers? Or not.

Am I able, in my context, to make full use of my gifts and talents, or are there barriers preventing me? Has how I feel about my context for ministry changed, or evolved in recent times? What are the challenges I face, and are there areas where I need to develop new skills? Where can I access the training, I need to develop?

Finally, the question of 'My Future', and this is certainly an area many colleagues are thinking about amidst all the change of Presbytery Planning at the moment. Is my changing context the place where I am called to be? Is it time for a new challenge? Do I feel confident in facing the current change before me, or are there new skills I need to learn? Do I feel called to this new Union or amended role? How do I balance the desire to grow with the anxiety about change?

The conversation should end with some points for action or reflection for the participant to take away and think some more on.

Although the rubric I've mentioned is there to help structure the conversation, in practice, as the conversation is participant led, fifty percent of the time it is disregarded, and the minister in question homes in on the question in their mind about their ministry, often whether or not they should remain in their context or move on.

It often takes them time to get to the nub of the question about the future they are wrestling with, because of their emotional connection to the people they are with, or because of sensitive nature of the factors that they are wrestling with – loyalty, relationships, expectations amongst other things.

In at least seven years now of facilitating these conversations I struggle to think of one where people did not quietly open up about their vulnerabilities or personal disquiet and challenges, and that is what makes it such a productive but also precious space for the facilitator to nurture.

At its best a Ministry Development Conversation can be the sacred space for someone to give voice to their deepest fears and longings about their call, and their relationship to the context. It can be the space in which they finally voice the change they have been mulling over for some time and how this relates to their own faith journey and relationship with God.

The challenge for the facilitator is not only to listen well, but also to reflect back faithfully to the participating minister and in ways that makes them further question assumptions made and certainties asserted.

Most ministers approach these conversations, naturally, when contemplating change, rather than having them form part of a regular and disciplined pattern of discernment.

I wonder if that speaks to our need to nurture a different culture in ministry. A culture that is more collegiate and where it's safer to open up to colleagues about our own questions around our role, our ministry and our future.

I wonder if the Church of Scotland needs a reappraisal of what its expectation of its ministers is, or should be, today? And whether it's realistic!

How can we encourage each other to be lifelong learners, and resource and invest in ministers and others to regularly upskill and learn new things, not only that they can grow in ministry but also so they can feel valued and invested in as people?

I wonder if congregations themselves need conversations facilitated by Presbyteries around these themes of call, context and continuing professional development. Would it not help them gain insight into the perspectives of ministry that many of their ministers have?

We begin our ministry with our call being tested and affirmed or not by the church at large. I wonder what place there is for some continuing dialogue around testing of call as the years in ministry pass by. Do Ministry Development Conversations fulfil this, or is there a need for a fuller process?

2C FILLING A VACANCY
From *Speaking from the Heart*

Ministers[31] of all generations have tales to tell of their brushes with Nominating Committees. The funnier the story is, the more it is probably an indictment of the standards of process some congregations see fit to use. As a probationer many years ago, I found myself in a small room being interviewed by three representatives of a rural charge I had not yet visited (and never did). The local Presbytery was in the middle of adjustment in the area, running that process bizarrely in parallel with the recruitment of the new minister. Now as a probationer I knew little about anything, of course; but I had a vague sense that something was wrong when the interviewers were unable to name the charge or state whether it possessed a manse. Such was the confused state of the adjustment process that here was a Nominating Committee earnestly trying to persuade a foolish baby minister to buy a pig in a poke.

---

[31] I have purposefully used random pronouns in this essay.

A more common error by far is the expectation by a vacant congregation of finding the perfect minister no congregation has yet had, or by the available minister of finding the Church of Scotland's only flawless congregation.

Finding a human minister

No amount of experience of past ministry seems to cure some congregations of the intention of recruiting a perfect minister, able to undertake a series of tasks so extensive that it would more than fill his or her waking hours. No amount of relevant experience in other walks of life seems to dissuade intelligent church leaders from expecting the next minister to lack the last one's flaw but have no other flaws of his own. No amount of leadership from the Interim Moderator or guidance from the Presbytery's Advisory Committee seems to break the determination of some to recruit to a job-description so detailed that it simply is not the Ministry of Word and Sacrament, a job-description that never includes 'just love them'. The risk is that the Nominating Committee is so attracted to the applicant who knows how to appear on first encounter to be exactly what they think they want, that they do not give close enough attention to the quirky, off-beat, unconventional minister, or even in some places just the female, foreign or disabled minister, the minister who will leave people wondering 'how did we do that, how did we get there, where did that miracle come from?'.

Nominating Committees have great fun and great success when they set their sights on finding a minister who is a fallen, fragile human being, someone so much like themselves that they can imagine being loved by him or her. Nominating Committees are excited by their work when they exclude no-one, who allow themselves conversations they would never have dreamed of with people they had never imagined. Nominating Committees take pleasure in saying to their Kirk Sessions 'you're not going to believe who the new minister is going to be'.

Requiring an acceptable minister

Committees can no longer declare their preferences in areas that are protected by anti-discrimination rules. Much as they would love to reduce their work by ruling out in advance those who do not match the desired age, sex and marital status, they are compelled to waste everybody's time by going through the motions of seeing everyone who applies, and then of finding a persuasive – or if not persuasive then at least technically legitimate – reason not to appoint them. They can, however, limit the scope of applications by specifying in advance the theological style they believe is the only acceptable one. With the help of an Interim Moderator who has played the game before, they produce an advertisement in code, which every other minister can read and use to select genuinely possible opportunities.

You might think that every minister has a Bible-teaching ministry, to some extent or another, in some style or another. Yet the use of the word 'Bible' in a vacancy advertisement usually sends the message that the congregation requires a minister from one end of the Church's theological spectrum. Or rather, it indicates that the Committee has decided that the congregation ought to require such a minister... which might come as a surprise to the congregation or not, depending on quite a few things. Conversely, the word 'inclusive' in the advert, describing the breadth of the congregation or its work in the community, is code for a liberal position in the debate on human sexuality and implies a welcome to those who are the subject of that controversy.

Whatever helpful nods and winks are given, they are based on the presumption that the searching congregation should set the terms, limit the search, determine who is or not to be given a realistic hearing. There is here a restriction on the potential for unexpected matches, and it is a restriction coming from one side of the communication, the side that gets to make the first move. It takes a bold minister to refuse to be put off by the signals, and to insist on applying anyway, perhaps genuinely or perhaps out of a gritty determination not to allow that part of the system to work. Half a generation ago, two female ministers serving together on a committee designing the Church's original anti-discrimination rules realised that a very prestigious city congregation (very prestigious according to itself, you understand, which is how these things always go) was in the process of advertising for a minister and was extremely unlikely to choose a woman. It was all they could do to resist applying and invoking their committee's new anti-discrimination instruments when neither (presumably) appeared on the short leet. But that, admittedly, would not have been a genuine application, however satisfyingly it might have turned out.

Congregations, wittingly or not, slice up the Church's ministry and advertise themselves to only part of it; and then they wonder why so few people apply.

Certainly, congregations are entitled to have certain core expectations of a minister. The University and Church will have educated and trained the candidate and allowed him or her to get to the point of ordination only on being satisfied that he or she can reasonably preach, administer and offer pastoral care, study and work reflectively, and interact with those with whom any minister is meant to engage. The universal minimum of the minister's job can reasonably be expected to be fulfilled by this person. What else is it fair to require?

The congregation, because no two are the same, will have its own particular life, ie elements of its own local mission and ministry, which surround that irreducible minimum. The question is: why does the field of possible ministers have to be limited by the peculiarities of the congregation's current activities? If those distinctive local priorities exist because the congregation has a passion for them, does not the congregation themselves undertake them? If they exist because a previous minister insisted on them, has she not gone? What strange and wonderful new initiatives might be unleashed on the unsuspecting community when the Committee has the courage or inspiration to do something that seems rather crazy? What much-loved traditions might be blessedly put to sleep to everyone's private relief? If the evening service were put out of its misery – attended as it is by a dozen people who all attended faithfully in the morning but feel they are supporting the minister by maintaining the burden of her writing another sermon every week – what else might be done with the time that is saved? What, in short, could be lost or might be gained if the job specification is freed from the terrible grip of current expectations?

And yet in reality congregations reduce the variety of applicants before their advertisement has so much as seen the light of day; and present a detailed mould into which the successful candidate will have to squeeze.

What does any such congregation look like to the outsider? What does it look like in the carefully crafted and beautifully printed parish profile? What does it look like to the local minister who will be phoned by potential applicants who have more sense than to rely on the profile alone? What does it look like to the Presbytery Clerk, who will be phoned by friends who are supervisors of probationers thinking of applying?

Seeking an ideal Congregation

Just as ministers can be expected to possess a common core of training and competency, so a congregation is expected to have certain irreducible resources. These will include physical things: a church building (but these days not everywhere), enough people to provide the standard functions of congregational life, and tools of the trade like organs, hymn books, communion ware and so on. The minister will naturally pay particular attention to the manse, and if he or she is lucky will discover that the fabric committee has adopted the attitude that the manse should be in exactly the state of readiness they would expect of their own homes.

There are congregations whose physical infrastructure is inadequate to the task, and yet they still puzzle over their failure to recruit a minister. A vacant congregation has failed to renovate its elderly church building during its last three ministries, while almost every other parish in that half of the Presbytery has refurbished, rebuilt or replaced theirs. No doubt they will have a sense of unfairness if they do not quickly recruit a minister; but who will tell them why?

Ministers will look too to the human infrastructure, the team of people, and want to know whether and how it works. The Session Clerk whose well-meaning interference has frightened away the last two young ministers, the united congregation who are so little united that the two groups might as well wear contrasting rugby tops, the former minister living half a mile away and cheerfully agreeing to funerals and weddings; these things shout loudly. Some withdrawals of applications speak very well of the wisdom of that minister; and they also say everything about the congregation that does not know itself well enough nor understand the game.

Only then, perhaps, if the congregation has survived scrutiny so far, does the applicant consider the job he or she will have to do. How many funerals per year? How many weddings per year? (How many *unavoidable, legitimate, parish* weddings per year?) How many schools, and how many of those inviting chaplaincy? How many care homes? How many Church of Scotland social care projects? What other churches, and what ecumenical expectation, burden or opportunity? What else is there that gives possibilities of all sorts: charities, community groups, political upheaval, twinnings (of church or community)?

There is a question a congregation can ask; the whole congregation, with Kirk Session and Nominating Committee and Interim Moderator and Advisory Committee and anyone else around who is willing to help them face the truth. Does this congregation *deserve* to have a minister? The answer will be 'no', if:

The minister will be expected to live and work in conditions the Committee members would not accept in their own homes and work;

The minister will be expected to take back tasks currently done in the vacancy by congregational members who are perfectly capable of continuing to do them;

The minister, for that matter, will be expected to do any tasks that could be done by others, including newsletter editing, driving, furniture removal, catering and photocopying;

The minister's spouse will be expected to do anything not expected of any other member of the congregation (and that presupposes that he or she happens to be a member of the Church and chooses to be a member of that congregation);

There is low-grade civil war amongst office-bearers, or unaddressed bullying on the broadest definition of it;

Any crying need has been unaddressed in the last three years, including the state of the buildings, the state of children's work, the distribution of jobs amongst office-bearers, the state of stewardship;

Anyone is foolish enough to declare, whisper or write 'The new minister will bring in young people'. (Don't, just don't.)

A vacant congregation with no shortage of money, talent and leadership had persuaded itself that it would be irresistible to the very best of ministers, and that the most articulate, experienced and well-known preachers of the Church would queue up to be considered. To be minister of the congregation would require the diplomatic skills of the Secretary-General of the United Nations, because there was just too much articulate talent, too articulate by half. A well-known minister found himself preaching there during the vacancy and spending some time after the service in conversation with elders and other members. Over coffee he found himself being backed into a corner of the Church building by the redoubtable Sir XY, who for years had pursued his pet projects so enthusiastically that they drained the blood from every other organisation and initiative in the place. By force of his personality and a capacity for the kind of lip-quivering disappointment described elsewhere in this book as disguised bullying, Sir X had everyone at his beck and call, and no-one could deny that he did very great good for very many people – even if the rest of the congregation was in a state of atrophy as a result. The visiting preacher left with two messages ringing in his ears. The first was from Sir X, that in the next ministry there would be no doubt that his projects must have the top priority because, goodness, they were so very deserving. The second was from some of the congregational leaders, that the preacher would be very welcome to apply for this charge that probably needed a strong hand and the ability to encourage and enable everyone's gifts. The preacher left in a fast car, not caring tuppence what the manse looked like or where his children would have gone to school.

A Future System?

History explains to us why vacant congregations have to recruit ministers as if they were businesses recruiting employees. For the first few centuries after the Scottish Reformation the minister was chosen by the patron of the parish, who might be the Crown, a local landowner or a burgh council. The local holder of power and authority chose the minister because that was who paid them. In the modern era, that system has rightly disappeared, but the congregation – once able only to veto the patron's choice – has stepped in to that vacuum to become the choosing body, through its elected Nominating Committee.

Perhaps that is an accident of history that should be questioned. Other denominations do it differently: churches with individual bishops, or the Salvation Army with its strong tradition of rank, operate much more of a 'push' system, sending the minister to the place of their service. The Church of Scotland has almost entirely a 'pull' system, Biblically-based no doubt, where the local church calls its minister to them. Its weakness is that congregations seem to be just as imperfect, broken and inadequate as the individuals who enter the ministry, but it is the flawed congregations in whom is placed all the power to choose. It is like dating, but as if only one partner makes the final decision. Must this be?

What would happen if, on the day that pigs fly, the system could be inverted?[32] Try this.

Ministers and probationers would make themselves available through a central system of intimation of availability, accessible only to the elected congregational Committees. There would be no need for individuals' names to be used, and no intimation of age, sex, marital status or any other issue protected by anti-discrimination law. They would be free to indicate their style of ministry, theological preference, or any other information that might help them to find an ideal match. Ministers could make themselves available to engage in due course with vacancies whilst remaining anonymous in these earlier stages. The congregations' Committees would now be the applicants, allowed each to have only three applications live at any time. A six-week period would be permitted for the usual process of meetings, hearing the individual conduct worship, and so on, but with the individual taking the lead.

And then the ministers/probationers would choose their preferred congregations. The decision would be made in consultation with the people who would be most affected, the people with so little influence at present, spouse and children. After all, no-one in a congregation will have to change their paid employment when the new minister comes; but the minister's spouse might. No child in the congregation will have to change their school when the new minister comes; but the minister's children might. No elderly member of the congregation will find their support package changed when the new minister comes; but the minister's elderly mother might. And the minister would choose the congregations that deserved to have a minister, deserved to have this minister.

---

[32] At the end of this essay I describe the day the pigs flew.

The new system could overcome another of the most frustrating aspects of the existing one. Nominating Committees currently each work to their own timetable, different by a few days from others progressing at about the same pace, but handling applications from the same people. Too often, an applicant's second or third choice congregation makes an offer of nomination with a tight time-limit imposed for acceptance, too tight to make it possible to wait and discover whether one's first choice of application has succeeded. On this imaginary new system, the intimation of available probationers and ministers would be made at a single point, and the interested vacancies given a time frame on which to work. On a pre-arranged date when all the usual process had taken place, the individual would state to the central co-ordinator of the system his or her full list of preferences in order. Where two or more individuals had the same church as their first preference, that congregation's Committee would immediately choose between them, and the rest of the allocation would continue with the removal of those elements. There is still therefore a recognition that some charges are more popular and will therefore have some choice. Within a day or two the matching would be complete, and the arrangements handed over to the Presbytery for the normal process of call and sustaining of the appointment. Individuals who had not selected any congregation, or who chose only those congregations who had the luxury of taking the offer of another minister in the scheme, would start again on the next cycle six weeks later; and so would congregations who had not succeeded in selling themselves at all, and who if wise would put in some effort to produce a different result next time.

This exact system would not work; of course it wouldn't. A dozen technical and logistical problems would quickly bring it to its knees. The flight of fancy that produces it, however, has its point of departure in the current system that tells congregations they merit a power of hiring and firing. They need to think differently. I am only making a point in a silly way. But let me press on.

Could a 'Ministers Available' column in *Life and Work* ever contain adverts such as these?

Probationer minister, 20 years' prior experience in Social Work, preference for West Central Scotland, recent experience in UPA parish, reputation for developing people's campaigning abilities, seeks busy charge to absorb energy.
(No-one reading this knows that this probationer uses a wheelchair.)

Parish minister, ten years in current rural charge, family reasons for wishing to move to Aberdeen area, heavily committed in national committee work, seeks part-time parish with strong commitment to community involvement.
(No-one reading this knows that this minister came originally from another denomination in a Commonwealth country.)

Army chaplain, ordained six years, belongs to Evangelical Alliance, seeks charge with emphasis on expository preaching and commitment to overseas mission.
(No-one suspects that this minister is in fact a woman.)

And in reply might congregations each send an application to one of those individuals, with covering letters like these?

Dear Colleague,

We refer to your advertisement in the May edition of *Life and Work* and wish to be considered as the location of your next ministry.

St Matthew's Parish is located in the East side of Glasgow. Set in an area of general poverty, with a very high number of asylum seekers in the population, the Church has come to be regarded as a place of refuge for people of many faiths and none, and its energetic and mainly young congregation has had to learn a great deal of legal expertise to support the most vulnerable in the community.

The Nominating Committee feels very strongly that this should be the place where you exercise your ministry, and that the work of the congregation will find a sure foundation if you lead us. The congregation is willing to undertake to organise a rota to ensure that there is someone present in the Church centre through each day to support you when you are there or to represent the congregation when you are involved in commitments elsewhere, or to develop its ministry of presence in any way you suggest.

You are most welcome to attend worship in St Matthew's at any time, and you should advise us when it would be convenient for us to meet with you and answer your questions about our work and witness.

Yours sincerely,

Dear Colleague,

We refer to your advertisement in the May edition of *Life and Work* and wish to be considered as the location of your next ministry.

St Mark's was recently disjoined from its linkage with St Luke's here in the Mearns, and as a part-time charge has recovered its original single-centre ministry to the farming country to the south of the nearest small town. The parish area coincides with the catchment area of a Primary School, which lies within easy walking distance of the new-built manse in the hamlet of Markstown.

The parish church, originally built in 1545 and with Grade A listed status, attracts many weddings each year. These generate fees producing a large surplus over the Giving to Grow allocation that is therefore easily met each year, and the weddings are conducted by a recently retired minister living in the area and employed for this specialist ministry.

Our committee will be delighted to make arrangements for you to spend a weekend at a hotel a few miles away and to show you round the parish, church and manse. Your privacy is important to us, and we are proud of our record of confidentiality in our process to date.

Yours sincerely,

Dear Colleague,

We refer to your advertisement in the May edition of *Life and Work* and wish to be considered as the location of your next ministry.

Following the departure after thirty years' distinguished ministry of our previous minister, Dr D, on his appointment as Director of the EA's new Titus Project, we are anxious to help our next minister to discern their calling as soon as possible. In our times of prayer together the Nominating Committee has been convinced that we should be completely open to the guidance of the Holy Spirit and to the possibility that something new and beyond our attempts to control it might take place here at Smith Memorial Church.

With your experience in the army, working largely with unchurched young adults, we would be excited to meet you and discuss the concerns we have about teenagers in our parish, and the shape of our future mission to them in particular. This will of course be our task, but we know we need expert guidance, and believe you may be able to support us.

Our older members are particularly inspired by their energetic support of Tear Fund's work in central Africa and would like to find ways to strengthen those links and foster personal contacts with missionaries in that part of the world.

When you have had a chance to pray about this letter, we look forward to hearing whether ours is one of the charges you would like to consider further.

Yours sincerely,

2023 addendum

When the Presbytery of Orkney was working on its Presbytery Mission Plan throughout 2021 and 2022, previously narrated, we quickly agreed that we would be moving towards some sort of Orkney-wide team ministry. There was fierce debate about some of the details, of course, and lots of legal questions to be answered to make it happen smoothly. The main outline, though, was pretty obvious from the outset: ministers would belong to a county-wide team, and would each have a three-fold role encompassing a traditional worship-leading and pastoral care role in the community in which they lived, a similar role in other communities without resident ministers, and a wider role within the team doing the tasks that no longer needed to be duplicated and divided up.

As it happened, our manses were in pretty much the right places, and the number of ministers in post was smaller than the number allocated to us in the planning process. That meant that we did not need to move anyone from one place to another, nor did we need to end anyone's tenure to meet arithmetical constraints. All we needed to do was make it possible to redeploy people from time to time in the second and third of those three elements of ministry, to suit changing needs and assets over time.

All of this meant that, long before we had completed our PMP, there were some steps we could confidently take.

The Presbytery Mission Planning Implementation Group came through for us, allowing us to re-draft the conventional wording of a Basis of Reviewable Charge, so that it would point out that there was no need for us to invoke our legislative right to end a tenure (since we were not over-staffed), but to add in that right to tweak from time to time the details of a minister's job-description as necessary. And we adopted that as the universal form of tenure to be used in Orkney in any charge, and with immediate affect even before our PMP was approved.

And then we started recruiting to our vacancies (almost half our charges). We produced parish profiles on Microsoft Sway that were the Rolls Royce of advertisements, and we offered free trips to Orkney for anyone willing to come, but the kicker was that we required them to look at *every* current vacancy and not choose just one in advance.

And at that point, the 'congregation applying to ministers' dream I described in this essay became a reality in front of our eyes. The East Mainland knew that the people they were meeting were also meeting Birsay, Harray and Sandwick. Later, when the EM was filled, BHS knew that they were meeting people who were also spending a day in Stromness. Candidates returned to my manse for B+B chuckling at the wooing they had experienced, the lunches, the persuasive conversations. More than once such an enquirer ended up more interested in a vacancy that wasn't the one that had originally triggered their request to visit Orkney.

And in a Presbytery allocated 7FTE ministries in terms of the Act, and which at the end of November 2020 had 4 ministers (with two of those due to retire within about three years), we inducted a further 3.5FTE parish ministers inside two years.

Not so daft the daft dream, huh?

3A SEMPER REFORMANDA

So how do you take your reform: 'mata', 'mans' or 'manda'? For this section of our exploration of 'What the Church should be doing and How the Church should be doing it', I shall look at the nature of the process of change and reform in our Reformed Church and consider the different aspects on that process produced by three aspects of the very idea of 'reform'.

Sorry, but we need Latin

I hope the urban myth is true, of the exasperated elder who tweeted that 'we really have to get rid of all the Latin *et cetera* used by the General Assembly'. I wish I had the time to try to re-write one of these lectures replacing all the latinate vocabulary with Anglo-Saxon synonyms to placate that person. I would enjoy being a fly on the wall of the BMA if they debated replacing Latin and Greek anatomical and physiological terms, or sitting in on an attempt in the Scottish Conservatoire to re-write Byrd's Four Part Mass in English. I am constantly impressed by parishioners who never studied Classics at school but who rattle off the technical names of their ailments or refer knowledgeably to the generic names of their medications which they've learned by necessity. Learning Latin terms of art is a thing most people do.

Those who think that the process of government of the Church should shed terminology that happens to be cast in another language are essentially asking for that governance to be conducted using only words that are already known and understood; they are not considering the possibility that everyone involved might need – and might be perfectly willing – to learn a few terms of art to speed things along, just as you would do in many other spheres of life.

It really does save time. The new Church Courts Act had to give detailed definitions of what we used to call *pro re nata* meetings; and time will tell whether we will get ourselves into fankles when the process is abused because someone doesn't know the difference between the spirit of a *pro re nata* meeting and an *in hunc effectum* one – if a Moderator calls a meeting urgently which ought to have been called at the previous ordinary meeting but no-one knew that wasn't the same thing.

Rant over...

... but just for now, we do need to look at one word with three Latin endings, trust me.

Reformata, Reformans, Reformanda

Reformata is the **perfect passive** participle of the verb reformare (to transform or remould) and I would translate it 'having been reformed'. The implication of this is that the reformation has happened in the past, and that it was performed upon the Church by someone or something other than the Church.

Reformans is the **present active** participle and I would translate it 'reforming'. Here the performer of the action is the Church itself, and the action is assumed to be ongoing. I don't think I've ever come across the future active participle form in any theological text (that would be reformatura, and there is a small prize for anyone who can show me a genuine example of that term in any ecclesiological literature).

Reformanda is the **future passive** participle (sometimes referred to as a gerundive) and I would translate it as 'going to be reformed', or even 'due/requiring to be reformed'. This is the version that follows 'semper' in its common church useage, which is what I suppose gives it that implication of 'always [needing] to be...' Grammatically, the distinctive 'nd' element is performing the same function as in 'graduand', 'ordinand' and 'Reverend'.

In this lecture, I shall give some examples that spring readily to mind of moments of change and reform in each one of the Courts of our Church that might be characterised using these different nuances on the concept of reformation. I expect to conclude that it is the last of these, *reformanda*, that is indeed rightly the most important focus of that discernment by the Church that the previous lecture explored.

The General Assembly

Reformata
In my ministerial lifetime the General Assembly has added to its activities, corrected, spoiled, extended, contracted and many other verbs forbye. Those who have introduced the changes have probably done so prayerfully, and believe they were God's doing; and other people may or may not have agreed that's how it looked. We have a habit of seeing God's agency in the things we think are good and right, and otherwise not, don't we?

I have two favourite reforms, and one pet hate. Yours will be different.

In a distant age more brutal than today's, disciplinary cases were heard by the General Assembly itself, often at the end of a long day of other debates and therefore in sessions that stretched into the wee hours. Hundreds of ill-qualified ministers and elders, hearing only as much evidence as could be endured in such an arrangement, made decisions that could have the most far-reaching pecuniary impact on manse families.

Today, instead, small tribunals, with professional legal leadership and applying rules of civil procedure, sit to hear cases properly and confidentially, reporting in written form only what strictly needs to be reported as diligence to the Assembly. That is reform, compassion and justice holding hands.

The other reform was as curious as it was welcome. In the person of Alison Elliot the 2004 Assembly elected its first female Moderator; and a fuss was made about that. Since deaconesses had not been full members of the Court, and women had been neither ministers nor elders before modern times, a woman in that chair had been possible for less than a generation, and when it happened it was high time.

I rejoiced less in that, though, than in the fact that Dr Elliot was an elder. (It is a fun experiment to gather Scottish Church historians together and ask them whether anyone had ever been Moderator as an elder before. They are likely to focus on George Buchanan, tutor to the future James VI and I. Was he there as an elder, or a doctor of the Church which is an old category we no longer use? We have to say Alison was the first elder for 'at least a very long time'.) The curiosity, though, was that no Church legislation had had to be amended first to make it possible; it was as if the institution subconsciously knew the appointment of an elder had been possible all along, without having consciously noticed and exploited the potential of it for centuries.

As another example of something being legally possible but not practically recognised, some commentators point to the legislation authorising the ordination of women in 1966 (as elders) and 1968 (as ministers), which to a sympathetic eye reads as declaratory more than performative ie *stating* their eligibility rather than *conferring* it. Do you call it reform when a Church wakes up and notices what it could have done long before now?

Reform is not necessarily improvement, and that's a very important thing to remember, in order to avoid reform for its own sake. My 'pet hate' reform was 'Heart and Soul', a well-intentioned showcase event in Princes Street Gardens on a weekend afternoon during the General Assembly, which ran for about ten years. There was nothing wrong having congregations and agencies of the Church and its partners display their wares and try to drum up interest in the course of a fair-like event (it was unkindly referred to by some as 'tea in the park'). I had three problems with it:

It was more attractive to some people than the General Assembly it interrupted, while being less important in its task.

It was attended by the wrong people (the commissioners to the Assembly who already knew of the work of the Church if they had read their Volume of Reports and not the wider public who needed to be educated about our wonderful work).

It suffered from those two problems because it was held in the one week it shouldn't have been, distracting central staff for (some of) whom Assembly week is already a time of particular stress.

Reformans

When the Church constantly tinkers with something, it exudes a sense of unease. When the Church constantly tinkers with something, it suggests to me that the changes are more human than divine.

Often tinkering is perfectly right and proper. A major new process, like the latest version of the discipline of ministers I have mentioned or the radical exercise in mission planning we have begun to use, does not perfectly survive first contact with Presbyteries and congregations; it will need a snagging exercise perhaps over several years.

The unease comes when the Church seems to be grappling about for an answer to the same question over many years. The most dramatic example is the regulation of the moderatorship: both the election of a Moderator, and the expectations of their year. In the 27 years between my first arrival as an Assembly Clerk and writing this text, there have probably been changes to the rules in more years than not. The changes, notice, have normally addressed the electorate (the constitution of the Committee that nominates an individual), the duration of the role (whether one year or longer), and the support given (most recently the attention has been on housing, budget, training of Moderators' chaplains). It is as if the Church is circling round the question it cannot quite answer: what is this person to do?

What if – and indulge me here – we adopted the kind of minimalism I wish our Courts would adopt? What if the Moderator did what it said on the tin, moderated the debates of the General Assembly, put his or her name to any documents or statements that had to be made on behalf of the Assembly in the course of the year... but went back to his or her parish, chaplaincy, lectureship or Kirk Session membership at the end of May, being available for emergencies by the wonders of modern electronic communication or in person for the really, really big contingencies? What if our Committee conveners did the representation thing, providing that continuity over their four years that some feel is missing from the Moderator's single year in office? What if our new Presbyteries' Moderators were each seconded for 0.25 of their time to provide the gracious VIP visits to congregations and community organisations within their bounds?

My point is: when the Church footers about with something too much, something is up, and I strongly suspect it is not the breath of the Spirit.

Reformanda

Somebody, or perhaps that should be some *body*, needs to look forward into the Church's future and see what are the things that need to be corrected. And they need to do it constantly and not as a finite exercise. What are the pages of our book that just keep curling over, and have to be pressed flat over and over again? What are the fences round our land that will not keep doing their job if we neglect them, but have to be maintained every year? Who are the children who keep needing to be reclothed as they grow, or the old people who need to be re-clothed as they shrink a little?

The correcting, if we are serious about our Latin or rather our heritage, is not done by us reflexively, but done to us by God. And that gives us the frightening truth that the reforms we need will not necessarily be those we think we need.

This whole volume might be said to offer an important object of that kind of 'reformanda': the means of discerning the will of God for the Church. If that is focused only on governance itself, it will be tricky to avoid circularity (how do we find out how we need to be changed by God so that we are better at finding out how we need to be changed by God?), but that does not excuse us.

Focused on the wider, substantive work of the Church, 'semper reformanda' must mean the slaughter of sacred cows that look a lot like buildings, ministries, and even principles and minor articles of faith. That is why I am so irked by the ceaseless stream of bright new little things someone in authority thinks I have time to do; and so I reduce, like a sauce, the Remits Booklet that emerges from each year's Assembly. It is because I know, semi-consciously most of the time, that there are bigger things to put right for my congregation and for me.

Presbyteries

Turning to the middle-ranking, and arguably archetypal court of our polity, what examples can you give of Presbytery reform that seemed to be godly at the time but done and dusted (reformata), or constantly worked at by the Church as a human institution without prospect of escape from the process (reformans), or requiring us to throw ourselves open to the present and future direction of God's Spirit (reformanda)?

Reformata
My first example refers back to the root-and-branch improvement of the Church's disciplinary system mentioned already. It happened in two stages. The first, thank God, was that removal of the hearing of cases from the General Assembly and the substitution of a proper system of what we now call tribunals. In common parlance you would say the deeply flawed identity of judge and jury was addressed. But still the other key function in the process, that of investigation and prosecution, remained with Presbyteries, with the extremely mixed economy of large and small Presbyteries, Presbyteries that happened to include legally-trained members and those that did not, Presbyteries with Clerks who knew the Church inside out and those whose Clerks were willing volunteers expecting the job to involve a bit of minute-taking and a bit of administration and correspondence and certainly not expecting to have to act like a lawyer.

I recall chairing a small, obscure disciplinary process inside one of the departments of the Church's work (ie not the discipline of a minister). The case was brought by a very large Presbytery, represented before our panel by two highly articulate and legally knowledgeable individuals. In a coffee break when parties had withdrawn, the panel members looked at each other and said, 'Thank Goodness this has come from Presbytery X; if it had come from Y or Z (naming much smaller Presbyteries) they could not have coped.'

In 2018 the Assembly enacted its new Discipline Act, the second phase of reform, which has completed the centralisation of that former Presbytery role, so that cases are still brought in the name of the Presbytery but handled by experts who are normally selected from the staff of the Church's Law Department. At the time of writing the Assembly has asked for the last piece of the jigsaw – the Complaints Process for situations that do not fall under the Discipline Act – to be examined with the same sort of scrutiny.

The argument I am making throughout this lecture about an attitude of 'ecclesia reformata' is that it is dangerous ever to believe that improvement is complete or will soon be complete. There is an interesting twist to this topic. With the creation of the new larger Presbyteries, staffed much more substantially and supported in their legal responsibilities from the centre, the current debate is whether it might be safe to restore to Presbyteries some of the disciplinary powers removed from them. Presbyteries Y and Z in my little story no longer exist; perhaps it is safe once again to operate the kind of philosophy of subsidiarity that so many true-blue Presbyterians nurture in their hearts.

Reformans

I resisted the temptation, in discussing the General Assembly, to illustrate 'ecclesia reformans' by describing the endless re-structuring of the central committees and agencies of the Church. It is, however, the bane of Presbyteries' lives, because the committees (and their Conveners and Clerks) in Presbytery are anxious to align as efficiently as possible to their opposite numbers in 121, while at the same time also aligning as helpfully as possible to the shape of congregational and Kirk Session life coming at them from the opposite direction.

As we witness at national level the final union of the historic departments known long ago as Ministry, National Mission, World Mission and Church and Nation into the one Faith Action Programme, we wait with (not very) bated breath to find out whether the reality of it is truly a single body with a number of programme streams, or rather all the old departments as clear as day with some sort of coat-holding mechanism co-ordinating them into the appearance of integration.

Entertaining and intriguing as that may be for Church polity watchers, it is a difficult question for Presbyteries. No-one in any Presbytery has time to serve on the regional equivalent of something as huge and amorphous as the Faith Action Plan Leadership Team.

So let us hope the goalposts stop being moved for a while, and our structures find a little peace, and leave us in that peace to get on with the more important reforms we are called to bring to fruition.

Reformanda

Though it may sometimes feel to the humble parish minister as if the Assembly is willing to heap more and more routine tasks onto his or her head year by year, that is presumably not the intention of the Holy Spirit. Unglamorous though it is to propose a reform that is not some exciting* new idea or initiative or programme, I believe that Church people need to preserve each other's mental health by finding the courage to reform things by ending them.

What are the activities that are flogged over and over again with results that do not justify the effort? What are the outreach activities that salve the consciences of those who put hours of effort into them but make no difference? What are the special services designed to be attractive to those who never come near them, and only achieve the alienation of those who feel infantilised by them?

But what a feeling of relief floods through a Kirk Session when it no longer has to struggle over a building. What a blessing it is to the Sunday School teachers who are able to attend adult worship for the first time in years because something else, well away from Sunday morning, is designed for the small number of children associated with the congregation.

I mention this in the context of Presbytery life because our new united Presbyteries are settling into new routines and programmes. Let those not be the sum of the activities of their predecessor-Presbyteries, the same burdens and 'aye-beens' and oppressive habits.

(*Just while I'm here, may I take a pop at the over-use of the word 'exciting'? It is invariably used in Church circles to indicate that the writer expects the reader to be excited by the writer's message, the initiative they are describing or the event they are advertising. I will decide whether you have excited me, thanks. If you must, begin 'We are excited to announce...'; but really, that's your limit.)

Kirk Sessions and Congregations

Kirk Sessions sometimes look a little like Ronnie Corbett in the Cleese/Barker/Corbett sketch 'I look down on him...' Subordinate to Assembly and Presbytery, it is all they can do to scramble their way through all the instructions and urgings that pour onto them from on high, whilst maintaining their fabric and finances against almost impossible odds. The idea that the Session could be an agency of change and reform is unlikely to be at the forefront of most elders' thinking. It should be.

Reformata

It's safe to assume that the number of congregations going through appraisal and adjustment in the mid-2020s is much higher than it has ever been. It is always a great relief to get to the end of any painful procedure, and when Big Brother Presbytery has finished inflicting the outrageous and unwelcome union or linkage (or whatever), that understandably feels indeed like the end of something horrid.

If Kirk Sessions can find that extra little bit of stamina and patience, to regard the date of adjustment as being the point at which reform begins – not its end-point –, the congregation will escape the constriction of thinking it is 'reformata' once and for all. Instead, it will be open to the glorious craziness of stopping the old and discovering the amazing new in personal spirituality or community engagement or a concept of mission that really means something to them in their time and place.

There is another point that is mistakenly regarded as an ending, the end of a vacancy with the beginning of a new ministry. That collective sigh of relief, which to the newly inducted minister sounds suspiciously like 'there you go, you have it now, we've had our turn', sinks the heart. The congregational leader who says instead, 'Is it OK if I carry on doing the task I picked up when the last minister left?' is the true saint of Christ's Church.

Wouldn't it be fun to ask every member of every Kirk Session, every year, to complete the sentence that begins 'In the Church somebody needs to...'? It would only work if they were promised that *they* would not immediately be asked to be that 'somebody', as they might be thinking of something they are not especially able to lead. The ideas would be varied and some of them would be wild. The resulting activity would be a force-multiplier of the work currently done by the few (in some places, the very few). The resulting philosophy, surely, would break the perceived link between inducted ministry and congregational progress, because so much would be advanced by so many.

Reformans

When congregational reform consists of human agents trying to steer their congregation towards their human visions, they tend to default to the limits of that vision.

Conduct a rigorous Local Church Review that prises out of the Kirk Session its deepest desires for the future, and it may sound a little like the Church of the 1960s. Most of the elders were small children in vast Sunday Schools back then, in days when it took more courage not to be churchy than to knuckle under and turn up. Everything was the other way up from the Church of today, and wouldn't most of our leaders love to wake up tomorrow in a world back like that one? The adjustments they will make to congregation life will aim for that utopia, because that is the model of 'success' or 'obedience' or 'mission' that seems unarguable.

But it is attempting to reform the Church backwards, into a different social, ethical, patriarchal, heteronormative, imperialist... need I go on?

Luther's 1517 dictum 'Wo Christus ist, geht er allzeit wider den Strom' ('Where Christ is, he always goes against the flow') is a breath-catching standard for those attempting to follow him. What would be the last thing anyone expects of the Church whose past they have long since rejected, whose historic patterns are what they dread most?

It means, returning to the most painful topic of all, holding assets as lightly as possible, seeing buildings, money and traditional local appointments as agents in the service of the greater purpose, of that mission which this lecture-series pleads for the Church to discover afresh and anew and afresh and anew and afresh and anew.

That word 'discover'; maybe that is the simple difference between 'reformans' and 'reformanda', for it points to the difference between what we construct in our own imaginations (and then tinker with because we viscerally suspect it's not quite right) and what is revealed to us from beyond our individual and collective calculation so all we are doing is discovering it.

Reformanda

In the early days of the Church's concept of Pioneering Ministry, one of the most interesting and ingenious applications of the idea was a ministry to the farming community in Ayrshire. This replaced a ministry based on geographical territory with one based on economic community, and it allowed an element of specialism in pastoral care. It seemed to hover somewhere between chaplaincy (which nowadays is rarely provided directly by the Church of Scotland, but mainly through the receiving agencies as employers) and traditional ministry.

The new Presbytery Mission Plans can include any number of appointments that are not conventional inducted parish clergy. The Team Ministry in Shetland consists only half of parish ministers, and even they work creatively in that team and not wholly in geographical silos. Every time a Presbytery discerns the opportunity for something that had never been conceived of in the Church's past, the Church changes a little, engages a little more with the world we serve. It will require a letting-go attitude amongst parishes and Sessions that must lose their more traditional expectations so that the new thing can be resourced from finite assets.

Here is a scenario for a Kirk Session discussion sometime. Ask them what are the things about the local Church that they would describe as 'ours'; when, in meetings and planning discussions, they have used the word 'our' in framing a position about anything; and whom they mean by 'us' in those moments. Ask them what would happen if 'our' and 'ours' were banned in spoken and written language for that congregation, so that every pound of investment, every brick in the buildings, every hour of ministerial time, every bit of volunteers' energy, was given unbounded, unowned, unlimited. Where would that take us?

Conclusion

There is one more lecture in this collection, as well as some further materials from the guest contributors to the University course that gave rise to this volume, companion material from *Speaking from the Heart* and other shorter illustrative pieces. That final lecture – 'Bearing Authority's Burden' – (chapter 4A) turns from the task of the Church to the tasks of the individual who is involved in the running of the Church. It is more of an advisory piece for occupants of seats in Church Courts, a different kind of text from what has gone before.

And so at this point, I suppose, the arc of my main argument about the Church is complete, and here is what I think I have contended.

In Lecture One (Missio Dei: Missio Ecclesiae) I have argued that the current project of the whole Church of Scotland rests on a concept of mission that does not bear the weight that has been put on it and was not produced by the whole Church properly. It fails to address the principal need of members of the Church to be developed and nourished as spiritual beings, and it fails to give adequate weight to worship as a primary activity of the Church. Or at least, it fails to respect the equal rights of those who do not happen to subscribe to a model of mission that privileges outreach above those other things. That the model is vague is my personal opinion; but that it fails to be inclusive of the purposes of the Church is a conclusion I believe is widely held.

I concede that I do not pursue that argument to find a better definition. Instead, I ask how the Church as a whole goes about finding it.

In Lecture Two (Corporate Discernment) I ask what is the corporate equivalent of all our individual prayers for discernment of God's will. It too is certainly prayer, but the marshalling of the thoughts of many into a spiritual event adds a very complicated stage to the process, compared with me sitting down each morning in the study and asking God what's expected of me... I suggest that the Church needs to disentangle the tyrannical 'Urgent' from the obvious 'Essential' and the easily missed 'Desirable'. She needs to ensure that the responsibilities of administration do not smother the birthing of new policy ideas. And she needs to get rid of every scrap of unnecessary activity, so that we all have space for new callings.

The Church needs to do these things because she is a living organism, which by definition means a changing one.

So in this third Lecture (Semper Reformanda) I have offered lots of examples of reform I have witnessed in the course of my very mixed-up ministry, and suggested that we must constantly be on the alert for apparent reform that appears complete or seems to be more pushed forward by human institution than drawn out of us by God's Spirit. Apart from the implicit plea for theological educators to drill the proper meaning of 'reformanda' into our students' heads before we unleash them on the Church through ordination, the stories in this lecture are intended to 'excite' the readers – but of course I would never assume I had succeeded in that! –, excite you to wonder what lies ahead for our Church.

3b CONTRIBUTION FROM FIONA SMITH
PRINCIPAL CLERK, GENERAL ASSEMBLY

'A Big Beast"

The Kirk may be today a shadow of its former self in terms of its status and influence upon the Scottish nation and its people. Nonetheless it remains a big beast of an institution. But how can an institution whose polity and structures were birthed in the 16th and 17th centuries speak to and deliver the Good News of Jesus Christ to the fast paced, ever-changing world and diverse people of the Scotland that we live in today?

Can a conciliar system of governance, where authority and decision making are diffused, ever be fleet of foot enough to discern, agree and implement effective plans for mission and ministry today, let alone the future?

The evidence of the huge decline in the Kirk's membership over the last 50 plus years and the resulting future predictions that by 2050 there will be no one left suggests that the 'Big Beast' can no longer deliver the goods.

No wonder we have in recent decades grabbed on to the Reformation principle 'Ecclesia semper reformanda' with all our might as we have initiated new structures, new ways of planning, and new ways of being church to halt not only our decline but our demise. After all our foundational principles are that we are to be a church that is always reforming – a church on the move.

Since 2021 we have coalesced around the word mission all agreeing that mission is what we should be about and so everything must be viewed through that lens. However, there is no one all-encompassing definition of what mission is or what it should look like which is hardly surprising given the diversity of theologies and traditions that make up the Kirk.

Nonetheless, Presbytery planning is now termed Presbytery mission planning. Its noble aims are to address all the issues we have kicked down the road for decades, such as, the lack of ministers of word and sacrament as well as the material consequences of our disruption history that has meant in many places across Scotland we simply have too many buildings.

This has been and continues to be a difficult and painful process that has resulted in the courts of the church clashing as the one or the other is blamed for making wrong decisions or for overreaching their authority and power.

Its always someone else's fault.

Poor old Presbyteries squashed as they are between the Big Beast of the General Assembly and the Kirk Sessions on the ground bear the brunt of peoples' anger.

As indeed does that place called 121.

It is as if somehow the church offices are filled with bean counters who are not really part of the church, because they are too like the secular world, peddling burdensome compliance with civil law that has no place within the rarefied spiritually independent sphere that the Kirk inhabits.

Then we have the General Trustees whom we don't really understand where they fit into the colossus. We do rate them very highly when they give us some money to refurbish our building but we dislike them when they suggest our building should be closed!

All is however not lost.

Presbyteries are being reformed – larger, better resourced, and professionally run, they will now be equipped to tackle the plethora of challenges we face more efficiently and effectively. At least that is the noble aim but the reality is still very much work in progress.

No wonder then that increasingly the criticism being levied at the Kirk from within is that all these structural reforms are no more than the Big Beast rearranging the deck chairs on the Titanic.

Now don't get me wrong, structures do matter, but while structures can be liberating, empowering and enabling they can also be obstructive, needlessly bureaucratic and even oppressive.

Liberation theologians like Gustavus Gutiérrez's in the early 1970s brought that reality into the light when they began to speak of 'structural sin'. What they identified within the systems of the world in terms of politics, the law, governments, and global economics was that they can and of themselves create, both consciously and unconsciously, the conditions by which human beings individually as well as collectively are treated unjustly and oppressively.

From this we understand that it is not enough to just deal with the detrimental consequences on people's lives it is also vitally important to address the source of the problems. Desmond Tutu often used the parable of the river to highlight this truth:

"Late one afternoon a villager was down by the river when she noticed there was a wee puppy struggling in the water – the villager rushed in to save the young animal.

The next morning other villagers were down at the riverside when they saw two puppies bobbing up and down and so of course they jumped in to rescue them too.

Every day this just kept happening and more and more puppies were being rescued from drowning in the river.

The elders of the village called a crisis meeting – what were they going to do they could not keep on rescuing the puppies because they simply did not have the means to look after any more.

Then one old wise woman quietly said: we need to go up the river to its source and find out why these puppies are falling into the river in the first place."

So what do we find when go upstream?

The source of the Kirk is Jesus Christ, the visible likeness of the invisible God:

'For in him all things were created: things in heaven and on earth, visible and invisible, whether thrones or powers or rulers or authorities; all things have been created through him and for him. He is before all things, and in him all things hold together.' (Colossians 1: 16)

Christ calls each of us to trust in him and be united in him. Faith means trust. This is our common calling: to trust in Christ and to follow Him – to be the Light, His Light, shining in the darkness of this world with the values of the Kingdom of God all for the sake of others.

As we are individually united to Christ it means we are also united with one another who proclaim Jesus is Lord – together we become His body here on earth – the Church with Christ as our head. All authority in the Church and in the world, even if the world does not recognise it, comes from Christ who gifted us with the power of the Holy Spirit which brings us truth and grace.

The fundamental point is this: Our faith, our trust in Christ only has any real meaning in our lives when we live lives of trust one with another. Without such trust within the Body of Christ we become like any other human organisation. Without such trust no amount of re-organisation or re-forming will bear fruit.

Presbyterianism has long been described as 'institutionalised distrust' – like all good jokes it's the ring of truth that makes it funny! But when the laughter dies down maybe we need to stop and take a long hard look at ourselves and ask ourselves this: do we really trust in the Lord and his promise that he is with us and will equip us for the road ahead?

Are we willing to take the risk and trust one other because if we can't then what does that say about our faith?

'It helps, now and then, to step back and take the long view' – begins the prayer attributable to Oscar Romero.

'The Kingdom is not only beyond our efforts; it is even beyond our vision.

We accomplish in our lifetime only a fraction of the magnificent enterprise that is God's work.

Nothing we do is complete, which is another way of saying that the kingdom always lies beyond us.

No statement says all that could be said. No prayer fully expresses our faith. No confession brings perfection. No pastoral visit brings wholeness.

No program accomplishes the church's mission. No set of goals and objectives includes everything.

This is what we are about.

We plant the seeds that one day will grow. We water the seeds already planted, knowing that they hold future promise.

We lay foundations that will need further development. We provide yeast that produces effects far beyond our capabilities.

We cannot do everything and there is a sense of liberation in realizing that. This enables us to do something and to do it well.

It may be incomplete, but it is a beginning, a step along the way, an opportunity for the Lord's grace to enter and do the rest.

We may never see the end results, but that is the difference between the master builder and the worker.

We are workers, not master builders; ministers, not messiahs.

We are prophets of a future not our own.'[33]

The future of the Kirk rests in the word fides – faith – trust Trust in God and trust in each other – even those, perhaps even especially those whose views differ from our own. How we

---

[33] www.romerotrust.org.uk

listen to each, how we embrace difference and how we discern together the path the Lord is calling the Kirk to follow is the light that the world beyond our walls is crying out to see.

Only then will the Kirk become once more what it is meant to be – the body of Christ here on earth.

Our Presbyterian structures and polity are not our cage: we are.

3C ORGANISED RELIGION
From *Speaking from the Heart*

In the congregations, clergy houses, theological colleges and fraternal groups of the Church of England or the Roman Catholic communion, the local bishop and the Church's hierarchy are never very far from conversation, part of the awareness of the worshipping community even when not present in person. A person – experienced, chosen, accepted, known – provides one convenient focus for the life of the Church in one area, provides a single point at which the authority of the Church is visible. When things go well, he or she is the focus of unity and a source of inspiration, an encouraging figure representing the broader Church to those labouring in one small space within it. When things go badly, he or she is the target of frustration and complaint, and at his or her door are no doubt laid some criticism that he or she deserves and much that he or she does not. The structure of the denomination is manifest in a person who relates to everyone who is striving to be the Church there and then, so their connection to the system is through a human relationship. This volume contains a brief reflection from someone occupying that unenviable role (chapter 4B).

In the congregations, manses, divinity schools and local fellowships of the Church of Scotland, no individual exists to fulfil that role, to draw attention to a single point of focus in the structure of our Church. In times of success, there is no one central figure to lead the celebrations. In times of frustration, people choose many different targets for their anger or blame. All the Presbyterian has is an organisation that can be pictured in several shapes and populated in different ways. Some visualise themselves in a series of concentric circles that has the parish church in the middle, with the Presbytery and General Assembly surrounding them with support, supervision, resources, interference, interest, demands, and other things thickly supplying context and meaning to the central, local activity. The Church Without Walls Report championed this image. Some imagine themselves in a different series of concentric circles that has the national Church in the middle, with Presbyteries standing closer to the core and parishes around the outside, receiving the support, supervision and all the rest as things sent out to them to stop them falling off the edge. Members of the Church who talk about 'the Church' in the third person, not realising they are themselves part of the institution, probably work with this model. Some think of the Church in layers, highly conscious of its court structure and aware that the Presbytery has power of direction over the Kirk Session and congregation, while the General Assembly has the ultimate determination of questions affecting everyone. And some intuitive souls see no structure beyond the people and visible activities of the Church, and do not recognise the need for any human system of rules, norms and authorities in the Body of Christ present in the world.

Presbyterians are fondly accused by other Christians of respecting organisation in religion more than others do, and of having a more developed polity than exists in other Churches. In ecumenical settings, the Reformed Church representatives are somehow expected to have a special concern for meetings, minutes, rules and protocols. It might be a flattering reputation to have, but it is not merited. Other Churches have as many systems as Reformed Churches do; there are methods for appointing clergy, disciplining church leaders, allocating resources, measuring success, training for tasks, no more in one tradition than another, only differently achieved from place to place. With no individual figurehead standing between the observer and the legal structures, no bishop representing all the authority that is stacked behind him or her, Presbyterians can simply see more clearly the whole of the machinery running the life of their Church, see unobscured the machine's glory and faults.

The Spirit and the Law

In every structured Church in every age there always exists a school of thought that opposes the structures, rules, authorities – the very organisation itself – to the movement of the Holy Spirit to achieve new and amazing things and to form and reform the Church without limit of human imagination. The first Desert Fathers left every structure behind and found a hermit existence free from every social constraint on their piety and obedience. Irish missionary saints set off with no support, utterly free to turn Europe on its head. Religious communities, from wandering friars to warrior Jesuits and enclosed mystics, were founded almost always by someone leaving the familiar and beginning again without their old rules. Still today on the edges of many communities of faith inside the Church of Scotland, people are bursting to express their faith in new ways without having to satisfy someone else's standards or defer to anyone who is not there, who does not see the Spirit move in this place, who is not part of the new movement, the new way of being the Church.

It seems important, though, to notice the logical flaw that imagines these are things that are opposed to each other. 'Organised religion' is not the opposite of 'spiritual initiative'. The opposite of 'organised religion' is only 'disorganised religion'. The opposite of 'spiritual initiative' might be 'spiritless initiative', and it might be 'spiritual inertia'. That is all. Whether a religious tradition is generally well organised or generally shambolic does not of itself determine whether the Spirit of God is present and whether change is possible. Good organised religion might provide the flexibility to seize signs of revival and hasten wonderful new things. Bad organised religion may stifle the most patently godly new idea, defend old ways relentlessly and do awful damage. It is the manner of the organisation, not the shape of it, that makes the difference.

The Church over the long reach of ages keeps the tradition of patriarchs and apostles, trying to arrange their world in obedience to the expectations God placed upon them. Surely the Old Testament follows the efforts of a people identified by a code of living, grittily maintaining difficult laid-down patterns of interaction with each other, with strangers and with God. Under all the provocation any life can suffer – rootlessness, famine, conflict, slavery, civil unrest – a race of men and women recognised its very point and meaning in a structure of regulation. The code was not an obstacle to their walk with God but marked its path. The Law was not a distraction from spiritual growth but its means. In the generations of Jewish history where the people managed to resist choosing a personality, a king, a human star, they saw their place in the world by looking at the way their life was shaped uniquely for them as for no other people.

And surely the New Testament tells the shorter, explosive story of a new way of living with God, which burst out of the old so vigorously that some custodians of the old way feared and resisted it and believed it was a canker that could not remain there. From the very hour that Christ sent out the Twelve in pairs with a rule of simplicity and a plan of campaign, until the Apostles thrashed out agreement about a relationship with the old law and used international letter-writing to direct church life all over the Empire, the embryonic Church developed means, standards, consistent practices to ensure its faithfulness and its effectiveness.

Today our Church never ceases from wrestling with those demands, asking itself endless questions about the requirements it places on its people, straining to know the commandments to follow and see the means to keep that faith. How can the guardians of religious rules provide the ones that are needed, recognise the ones that impede progress, and all the while avoid idolising laws that turn out to be the creation of human skill and the object of human conceit?

Leaders and Rulers

All this struggle it places into the hands of those who are chosen to make its decisions: ministers of Word and Sacrament, professional deacons, and the elders of the Church in every parish. Rightly our Church finds men and women of great talent and many kinds of holiness, and excitedly marks them as preachers, teachers, evangelists, pastors and workers in many difficult and specialist tasks. Unavoidably our Church pours all these people into the categories of minister, deacon and especially elder; it seems to be the obvious way to acknowledge and honour them, to place them in the community as givers of some particular service. The problem is that we tend to force all our charismatic leaders into governance. Imprisoning those gifted spirits in the Church's courts is unkind to them, and anyway it is wrong for the

Church. We need to have the courage to recognise that many of our best leaders do not need to be elders, that the eldership is not the only place to make a difference. Those whose authority equips them to recruit and ordain others to the eldership need the moral courage to confer that ordination only on those whose charism is one of leadership and governance. Ordination of elders is the sign of bearing one particular burden and one only, the steering of the Church and the structuring of her means.

Ordination is for leaders. Appoint, then, those who may visit the old and frail; appoint those who help to ensure the Church is a welcoming and hospitable place; appoint those who handle property and money and complicated things most people would rather were not their duty. Do not ordain these though, except those who are policy makers, judges, discerners and defenders of the way that all should follow. The number of leaders and governors God provides to any congregation really does not have to coincide with the number of districts into which the membership is divided for pastoral purposes; do not keep ordaining up to that number come what may. The number of leaders and governors God provides to a particular congregation might not be predictable in relation to its size, so do not feel you must ordain many elders only because the congregation is large. The right number is exactly the number of men and women who have the gift of such wisdom, experience and vision that they can be trusted to judge what demands should be made of other faithful people in living out the calling of the whole Church. Ordain only these.

Theirs then becomes a role that brings scrutiny and suspicion, that bears other people's hopes and conflicting expectations, that often takes them to a point where it is not easy to choose the future rightly. Once again, many metaphors abound: they are running a machine; or they are constructing the road ahead; or they are opening and closing doors; or they are switching on and off the sound of the Church's voice. They are, no doubt, themselves listening for voices and indications and calling and instinct, so that they will do the right thing, the godly thing, in any time of difficult decision. In the Presbyterian setting that has no focal individual, what they do will sometimes be the target of the disappointments of those who feel frustrated in what they are trying to do. When the rules for distributing resources fails the person fired by a new idea, and when the rules for retirement ages separate a minister and congregation who wished to continue together a little further, and when the rules about preaching do not allow a completely new voice to speak out a prophecy that is heart-felt, over and over again that suspicion arises, that the law of the Church, the government of the Church, the leaders of the Church cannot possibly be on the side of the saints.

Process and Abuse

And just occasionally that suspicion turns out to be right. In many Presbyteries, and in the General Assembly every year, some protagonists in the drama of debate abuse their good knowledge of process and procedure to achieve a technical victory over someone who is less experienced and sophisticated, and in so doing leads the Court to a hasty decision that turns out to be a bad one. A first-time commissioner at the Assembly is unaware of the Standing Order that says a motion involving new expenditure can be made only if a scheme for finding the cost out of the rest of the Church's central budget is also proposed. She has a dream, a religious passion, for a new project she can see would transform lives and encourage faith; and out of courtesy she approaches someone from the relevant committee to explain what she intends to move. The wily committee member says nothing about the Standing Order, knowing that the motion will fall foul of it and be ruled out of order by the Moderator. Luckily for the commissioner, her courtesy extends to providing the Clerks' table with a written copy of the motion; and when the Clerk notices the problem, she helps her to re-word the proposal in more general terms to survive the challenge from the committee. Serve them right.

In some courts, the body tries to operate with no skeleton at all, no predictability, no way of guaranteeing that everything necessary has been done, no tidiness in its conduct. A minister and Session Clerk have many beautiful ideas for the service to welcome new elders to their sphere of service, and they dismiss the all-too-familiar (they say) language of the Book of Common Order. Using inspiring and provocative language from another tradition, the minister commissions three members of the congregation to a new calling, but without the reading of legal texts or the putting of any vows he fails to ordain them. The three, and the whole congregation, are left feeling rather sad because the much-loved service of ordination – that would have so resonated in the memories of the other elders present – has been abandoned and no-one is quite sure whether the ordination has properly taken place. The passage of time, the elapse of the legal period to challenge its inadequacy, and as usual the grace of individuals to cover up the mess, takes care of it. Yet it never quite feels right.

In some courts rules and procedures are so excessively honoured by the organisation itself that the life of that body ossifies, becoming lifeless in the hands of fanatics. When a tiny Session of twenty members is run as if it is a cumbersome Assembly of 600, with the tiniest and least contentious decision put to a counted vote, the most sensible and welcome adjustment of wording minuted as a separate amendment, and the most helpful contribution ruled out of order because of some Standing Order about numbers of speeches, the Holy Spirit seems to be presented with a slalom to negotiate – which is not an ideal course for a wind blowing where it wills.

Process and Progress

If ever, though, there were a body that learned over time to grasp the spirit of good process but fend off all attempts to stultify it with minutiae, it was the National Youth Assembly of the Church. Hundreds of older teenagers and younger adults met each year to reflect on the most difficult challenges lying ahead of the Church, to elect representatives to the General Assembly, and to develop their skills as part of the up-coming leadership of the whole Church locally and nationally. The development of its ways was inspiring. The first two or three Youth Assemblies in the mid-1990s used actual General Assembly reports complete with actual Proposed Deliverances, were moderated by General Assembly Moderators, and probably flew straight over the tops of the heads of younger and less process-fixated members. These meetings were heaven for a few, while the rest no doubt enjoyed everything outside the debates. The next few Youth Assemblies, at the beginning of the new decade, still borrowed topics and suggestions from the General Assemblies' materials, but produced their own proposals, appointed Moderators from their own ranks, and found ways to involve far more of the members. It was still like walking a very strong dog, trying to stop those who loved the technicalities of debate from pulling everyone into the machinery they loved to play with.

Eventually the Youth Assembly found its way of working, entirely separate from the Principal Clerk's office. They tackled important themes they identified themselves, moderated by one of their own and clerked by another. They debated substance and knew how to avoid wasting time on details so tiny they could better be left to the General Assembly to fix. They produced a list of ideas the leadership of the wider Church wished they had not thought of, because they were so wise and difficult and sometimes irresistible. After the length of a generation the NYA reached the end of its arc of energy, leaving behind a legacy of several ministerial ordinations, a couple of marriages, and a stripe of Assembly-savvy youngish adults scattered around the Church.

From time to time the Courts of the Church catch that instinct and let the processes before them serve their mission. A minister, let us imagine, intends to retire at state retirement age. As the time approaches, she discovers that her adult son must undergo treatment for cancer and be cared for by her for six months. A change of circumstances and a house-move would be disastrous, and she is distraught. Surrounded by a loving congregation and a compassionate Presbytery, she discovers that an application is being prepared by the Presbytery Clerk for an extension to her ministry in terms of the regulations, along with another one for a compassionate leave of absence for the first ten weeks of her son's treatment. Everyone knows those rules were not designed for this, everyone, including every member of the Presbytery who unanimously approve both applications and offer to share the congregation's pastoral care for those months.

Or a congregation, let us imagine, is gradually losing its way and its new minister lacks the qualities of leadership needed to grip its difficulties and heal its malaise. Neither the situation nor the minister is so bad that the Presbytery could easily initiate any emergency action, but the Superintendence Convener is beginning to hear of the unease in the parish, to see more and more children transferring into his own neighbouring Sunday School, and to notice the slump in financial giving over the last twelve months. The rota for routine superintendence visits is due to be prepared for the coming year, and the Convener quietly slips the congregation to the top of the list, though it is not strictly their turn to be visited. More, after all, can be formally uncovered when searching questions are asked than by waiting for the situation to produce anything so brave as a complaint.

Or a tiny congregation has a Kirk Session that consists only of the minister and three elders. One elder is ill and the other two are infamous for their life-long suspicion of each other. The minister is at his wits' end and cannot begin anything new and creative. The Presbytery has used its imagination to find ways to bring the situation to its official attention, and the Business Convener proposes that two elders from the minister's other Kirk Session be appointed assessor elders to their neighbour for one year, to lift it off its feet by sheer weight of numbers and make change possible at last.

Flexibility and common sense extend to the guardians of the texts of the laws in the Church's administration, who relish the challenge to remove obstacles or invent new instruments of grace for the Church's work. They too are ministers and elders and members of congregations trying to follow the one who said 'follow me' without their feet being tangled in fascinating processes that only slow them down. Their gift at its best is the ability to think linearly as lawyers, and laterally as saints, in the same breath.

As narrated in chapter 3A, in 2000 the Church's Procurator designed a new system for the discipline of the few ministers who make misjudgements too serious to be ignored by the Church. (It has since been superseded by a further piece of legislation, but the story of the earlier one is instructive for my larger point.) A process emerged that passed muster with spiritual standards, human rights charters, Presbytery authority, people's perception of their own ability to handle such difficult cases, and best practice as then understood for hearing and adjudicating on evidence. In the ensuing years, as the first handful of cases washed through the new system like oil going through a new engine, the rough edges were gradually smoothed by many tiny amendments brought to the General Assembly by its Legal Questions Committee and approved on each occasion by the wider Church.

The process was – obviously – an uncomfortable, heavy endurance-test for those denying the allegation made against them, who had to undergo every part of the process in the legislation. It struck the Committee, though, that the experience was no better for ministers willing to admit all or part of the allegation and accept the censure of the Church without resistance. There was no abbreviated process in those cases, no motivation built into the process for people who might be persuaded to own up quickly to their ethical mistakes. What was needed was what the lawyers unofficially labelled the 'it's a fair cop' amendment, and no sooner was the omission spotted than it was filled. The procedure, still of course a horrible experience, became a much faster one for those who had already reached the point of admission and repentance, and deserved to be treated accordingly. Surely that is grace.

Process and Vocation

Facing ordination, standing on the brink of ministry, diaconate or eldership, the Church member has a tumult of thoughts crashing around inside: thoughts about spiritual adequacy and personal worthiness, thoughts about responsibilities to others and opportunities for service, thoughts about the routine ahead and the burden to be picked up in the coming days, and thoughts about all those rules and procedures and what is going to be expected. Those who are not lawyers are tempted to avoid all engagement with those latter things, either persuading themselves it is a distraction from the Gospel to focus on the Law, or just blanking it all out of fear of confusion or failure. Those who take a deep breath and apply themselves to discover how the governance works and how to make it work for good – and they quickly discover they do not need to be lawyers to achieve that – are the people who hold the levers of change throughout the Church. They are the ones who can make a business meeting inspire those who attend it; they are the people who can deal with a dispute quickly; they are the Presbytery officials who know how to speed up a vacancy; they are the staff members who can find resources to make someone's dream come true. They are the spirits who sometimes, maybe just sometimes, clear all those gates away from the path of the Spirit blowing through the Church and abiding by no human rules. It is the humans who make up the Church who will achieve very little in chaos, and who need all the help they can give one another to discover the ways that work.

4A BEARING AUTHORITY'S BURDEN

This lecture considers service in the Courts and governance structures of the Church. (For a reflection on the more general experience of members within our congregations, see the following chapter on 'Power in the Congregation'.)

At ordination, and in each subsequent induction or introduction to a charge or appointment, we Church of Scotland ministers take or repeat a vow about playing our due part in the administration of the affairs of our Church. Discerning what that 'due' part is, is one of the trickiest and most important tasks of ministry. It will not be the same for everyone, because we each have our balance of skills and abilities, and different contributions are expected from us in different areas of ministry, just as St Paul described way back at the beginning of the Church's history.

What *ought* each to do? The level of commitment to matters of governance ought to be greater in one minister (or deacon or elder) than in another. Some are best spared a burden they do not ably bear; indeed the Church may best be spared too in those circumstances. Others bring experience in law, business, administration, teaching and so on, and are used to running

Public and Third Sector institutions; it is easy to discern a calling to them to keep using those gifts in their new environment of Church life.

What *is* each in fact doing? To what extent is this individual stepping up to their plate? Some are very keen to spend lots of time on those tasks and embrace a large burden; some are less keen but somehow fail to avoid it; some have a talent for being unnoticed when the jobs are being handed out. If this lumpy, imperfect (but as yet unsurpassed) system of Presbyterianism of ours is to work, each of those types must feel equally vested in the work that is done, however much the finger-prints of an individual may show up on a policy, a rule, an initiative.

As a former deliverer of the Church Law training required of candidates for the ministry, I offer ten themes for discussion, which might in truth be ten pieces of advice for those training for ministry or recently ordained and getting the hang of our polity.

1 Employed or Ordained

It is still the case, for the moment at least, that our parish ministers are 'office-holders', as that is understood in civil law, rather than 'employees'. Until about a decade ago, the significance of that might have been that they were regulated in their work by Church Law rather than Scots Law, with a retaining wall of independent spiritual jurisdiction separating the Church's servants from other kinds of office-holders like police officers. Writing about this fifteen years ago[34] I was observing the Church on the verge of losing that privilege in any meaningful way – at least in relation to anything of any interest to those outside the Church[35] – and arguing for a pragmatic adjustment to an increasing subjection to the law of the land. Today it would be

---

[34] *The Crown Rights of the Redeemer*, Edinburgh: St Andrews Press 2009
[35] We retain our spiritual independence in relation to worship and doctrine – but who in Scottish society gives a hoot what we think or do about any of that? – so it's hardly a victory for us.

a brave Church lawyer who expected to have much success in trying to shelter the Church within an independent jurisdiction in face of an issue like employment.

But there remains a cultural difference, if not much of a legal one, between secular employees and the Church's office-holders. Somewhere, for every employee, there is a contract – written or perhaps implied – that determines the rights and responsibilities of employing and employed parties. And as in any contract, a material breach by one party absolves the other party from whatever their matching obligation would have been. An example is a contract for services from a trader: if I don't pay you, you won't have to do the work. For those of us who are inducted to our charges, by contrast, the relationship feels more like a covenant. And since that is a word that perhaps has as many definitions as occurrences, let me throw in here my definition of 'covenant' as a relationship of common obligation but where the promise has been made not only to the other party but also to God; so this time, where one party acts in a way that would have broken a mere contract, the remaining party in a covenanted relationship is not *ipso facto* released by that breach because the vows they took are still in force. An example this time is Christian marriage.

This means that I remain in my parish ministry until and only until I discern a fresh calling from God upon me to move, retire, or prioritise failing health. Being offended by the deeds of my Presbytery is not reason enough, unless I suppose the said Presbytery has made it impossible for me to function and fulfil my calling. It also means that I have a duty to work for the institution and its success regardless of my fondness for it or for the people I find in it. There's a challenge. In other words, the first rule is: No taking the huff and leaving.

2 Presbytery Polity is a Heartless Boss

I mean this apparently cynical comment only in a literal sense. Our polity is as 'personal' as that of Rome or Canterbury, but happens not to be vested in individual holders of authority (bishops); for us it is as groups of people structured into Courts and the agencies of Courts that we try to incarnate the authority of God within the life of the Church. We are not accountable to a single character, to someone with a single human heart.

The nearest we come to a Court having the personality of an individual is when a Moderator or Clerk imposes their particularly distinctive character on the style of its proceedings. Some of you will remember that moment in the Assembly when Ian McGregor, the twinkly nemesis of Assembly time-keepers, questioned the re-naming of some Presbyteries. Why, he wondered aloud (once he had completed his customary Gaelic preliminaries, of course), did we have a Presbytery of Dumfries **and** Kirkcudbright, and a Presbytery of Kincardine **and** Deeside, and yet his own was now the Presbytery of Lochcarron **hyphen** Skye? James Weatherhead, the Principal Clerk, without so much as a heart-beat's pause stood up at his desk and replied 'The hyphen represents of the new Skye Bridge, Moderator'.

But no, the real heart of a Church Court is a mysterious phenomenon when all the characters present bring all the results of the individual prayer already discussed, and there emerges from the debate a corporate sense of calling and determination and will, so that the Court acts with the faithfulness and passion you might ordinarily think only an individual could display.

The responsibility of the individual within that Court, especially perhaps an individual who is not the kind to stamp their singular character on proceedings like a McGregor or a Weatherhead, is to remember that they are as much part of the overall process as everyone else, and that the heart of that body of governance is in part the heart beating inside their own body.

3 Leading or Following

When a big decision slides silently through the General Assembly with neither an argument nor a vote, one of two things might be happening. On the one hand, these hundreds of commissioned ministers, deacons and elders may have been stultified into submission, overwhelmed by the forceful personality of the reporting Convener, rushed to judgement by a Moderator wanting lunch, or otherwise generally feel bullied into something that really isn't what they think is the right thing to do, but there is no time or opportunity – or no-one has the technical skill in the heat of the moment – to come up with a better alternative. On the other hand, what is usually happening – unspoken – is that the Assembly have seen the wisdom and common sense of the reporting Forum's members in suggesting this particular course of action, cannot improve on the detail of it, and feel no need to take up time debating what is obviously sensible when the time might be kept for something more controversial later on. The former characterisation comes from a more suspicious, untrusting mind; the latter pays silent tribute to the good sense and reliability of those who were entrusted with the topic by a previous General Assembly.

The buy-in to decisions of those who allow them to be approved is critical to give them meaning. I confess I have once or twice pleaded with Kirk Sessions not to approve an idea if every last elder in front of me is thinking 'Other people must be wanting this, so I won't oppose it but will just ignore it once we've moved on to other business'. A new initiative attended by none of the congregation's leaders because each thought the others liked it is just depressing. It is surely not too naughty an observation to make that every Assembly is presented with far, far too many 'sections of deliverance' (the technical term for each 'Instruct', 'Urge', 'Thank', 'Note' and so on); most of us in all but the largest of congregations can't begin to fulfil all of them. As I mentioned last time, after each Assembly I pick out the 'instructions' and any of the more passionate 'urgings' that I think will resonate locally, and take those and only those to my hard-pressed little Kirk Sessions for their action. I suspect that is not an unusual method of filleting all the hard work of central agencies and staff.

My point is that it is as much a form of service to receive and carry out the instruction of a Court of the Church as it is to be the person who attended the committee meetings, drafted the Report, framed the instruction and secured the budget to enable it to be done effectively and well. A lot of thought is required to be a follower too.

4 Making Policy or Obeying Policy

According to our Constitution, there are issues on which the Church is entitled to require its office-holders to adhere to a particular position; these are the beliefs that our denomination has decided are 'of the substance of the faith'. There are issues on which the Church permits liberty of opinion on those points that are not in that required core. And there are, inevitably, issues on which some disputants feel the Church ought to have a monolithic view imposed on everyone, while others are content with a variety of opinion. I have long assumed that genuine 'liberalism' in the Church has nothing to do with a person's opinions on particular contentious issues, but everything to do with an instinct to maximise the range of issues on which liberty of opinion is guaranteed.[36]

The art of being a Presbyterian is sometimes in identifying the moments in which it is permissible to express the minority view confident in the knowledge that the right to do so will be defended even by the majority. There are other moments, though, where the majority view has to be expressed even by someone

---

[36] See chapter 5, *From Scapegoat to Shibboleth*, for the most predictable contemporary illustration.

who privately disagrees with it. A minister who sincerely supports the concept of the nuclear deterrent has the right to oppose the many articulations by many Assemblies of a contrary position. Thinking very long and hard first about the necessary and likely effect of doing so, he or she has the right to express that personal view in the course of ministry and preaching, and certainly should not be pressurised – even by a Court of the Church – to take part in demonstrations that are quite counter to his or her own belief. But if that minister agrees to be a spokesperson for the Assembly, or serves as its Moderator, the personal voice is replaced with a corporate mouthpiece, and the task becomes a prophetic one on behalf of the official position of the Church.

There's a similar distinction to make between decisions that can be ignored and those that will be implemented even in the teeth of the most extreme unhappiness. If the decision relates to Presbytery Planning, then no amount of voting against (or abstaining, see below) will stem the tide of the practical application of what has been agreed by a majority. For heaven's sake, put up a fight at the point the policy is being made, if that is how you feel. And then work to make it work when you lose. Just don't mope; it's so draining.

The remainder of this lecture explores what that plea means in practice.

5 Test the Limits

When the wee boy said, 'The Emperor has no clothes on', we imagine him blurting out that truth without any great thought for the danger into which he might have been putting himself or his parents. Those who do the same in the hallowed halls of Church politics do not usually do so unthinkingly after a similar rush of blood to the head and unable to stop themselves. Presumably some of them say it knowing that at best they will draw a minority to their point of view and keep their consciences clear in the face of the daft determination of a foolish majority. And presumably others say it with a hunch that they will open a floodgate through which will pour everyone who has been looking at the naked Emperor and wondering who would be the brave person to say it first.

Once there was a solemn and earnest colloquium in the Church Offices thinking about Presbyteries and the way ahead. (I know, that doesn't really narrow down the timeframe because it's a perennial conversation, but that doesn't matter.) Round the table we went with all our ideas for the brave new things that Presbyteries should be doing to improve the mission of the Church. The invisible talking-stick arrived at a minister who at the time was probably one of the youngest people in any leadership position. And he said he thought that Presbyteries would be much better if they didn't try to do substantial work that would probably be done more expertly in 121 anyway, but instead Presbyteries should do the absolute minimum required of them in Church Law and let other agencies get on with the interesting stuff in other ways. Sadly, the meeting did not collapse in relieved agreement with him at that point; but it was an act of courage that changed the conversation just a bit.

Distrust momentum, because it may consist of nothing more than the failure of everyone before you to be the wee boy that first says 'But...' Have the courage to test the real mind of the meeting. If you crash and burn and the Convener is vindicated after all, you will not be victimised – or at least, not until you've done it several times and failed to ask yourself how good your judgement really is. If you succeed, you will have the thanks of a grateful silent majority all of whom are glad they didn't have to be the first penguin jumping into the shark-infested water.

6 Governance is not the enemy

Before I say something about how to be a nuisance, a thorn in the side of the establishment, and if necessary a loser, let me say something heartfelt about the way in which we cherish and support those we think constitute that establishment. I appreciate that in good management technique you should refrain from telling someone what their 'attitude' should be, and you should focus instead on more measurable actions. But this lecture is being read by praying people who, I guess, scrutinise their own attitudes, so this might be grist to that mill.

Most members of most Assembly and Presbytery Committees, and most of the Church's paid staff, do what they do because they share enough of your beliefs to belong in the same denomination as you, have a particular interest in or knowledge of their committee's remit, enjoy the trust of the body that appointed them to serve there, intend to do their best, and are possibly juggling the issue that is busting your chops along with dozens of other demands on their time. When they slip up, fail to understand the situation, forget to communicate some particular thing at some particular time, or make a decision that is so daft it should be overturned, no part of that last sentence stops being true.

Here is the thing about attitude: there is a discipline to learn of resisting bad decisions but not personalising debates. It is a habit to adopt of lifting the phone to the Convener or Clerk and saying, 'here is the good outcome I was trying to achieve; can we find a way to make it still possible?', or of inviting that mover and shaker to coffee to explain your needs rather than telling everyone else that you're never understood. You will never improve a situation by personalising it.

There are occasional exceptions, individuals whose tracing of a possible path from one influential post to a greater one distracts from the task in hand, or characters whose judgements are distorted by historic rivalries or offences. But happily the Courts of the Church, especially the General Assembly, have a mysterious instinct for seeing these things, an ability to spot badly-masked ambition, sleight of hand or wool being pulled over eyes; and in those moments a Court will say a courteous 'no' and ask for a different consideration or a further effort.

Securing a majority in a debate does not of itself constitute bullying. And losing a debate does not of itself prove that you were not heard.

That is only true, though, if the weaker voice, the loser in the debate, the questioner of the prevailing wisdom, is cherished too and not demonised. It is tempting, when you are secure inside the position of authority, to encounter the little boy trying to tell you the emperor is naked... but treat him instead as the villagers treated the little boy who cried wolf. The frequent complainer who never seems to 'catch 121 doing anything right' must not be assumed to be wrong every time; this umpteenth whinge might be the very time there really is a wolf approaching. The person who rarely says anything valuable still needs to be listened to, even if that takes time and effort. The invitation to coffee should be accepted; the extra ten minutes of meeting-time it takes to understand their situation should be gladly spent.

For if that respect is paid, then governance truly will not be the enemy, and we will strengthen this way we have of including in our decisions everyone who has ever been discerned as a leader figure (by which I mean all our ministers, deacons and elders).

7 Play your part

Once you have worked out what that 'due' part is, in terms of your aptitude, experience and qualifications, it is as much your duty to play that part properly as is anything else you vowed to do when you were ordained to any of those offices of leadership. What could be more important, after all, than assisting in the navigation of the very vessel that makes Christ's progress in God's world?

For those in professional ministry, the first step is to prioritise this work properly. It is a core part of your calling that has its place in your normal work-stream, not an accretion that adds stress on top of your 'real' job. That deeply difficult task we all have, of recognising what we do not have capacity to agree to do, involves resisting congenial opportunities closer to home in the parish if they would detract from our work for the wider Church – even if that is not an easy sell to our Kirk Sessions.

The next step is to accept appointments when asked, or to volunteer for appropriate tasks. There are some jobs that are attractive to lots of people, and others that lie on the bottom of the barrel because no-one really wants to do them. Might you be able to offer to do one of each, and hope others take the same approach so that everything is covered while everyone gets a little joy in their work? And when you decline something that isn't right for you, have a good reason, good enough that you would say it out loud; and have the confidence to believe the right thing might not be the first thing you're asked to do.

While you're at it, be active in nominating others for roles. We talk, in recruitment to our ministries, of the call that comes from the Church in support of the individual's sense of direct call from God. (The Church's discernment is, if you think about it, the basis of every non-accept decision made of candidates sure they have heard God's call.) That corporate discernment, discussed in the earlier lecture, continues throughout a ministry; someone needs to articulate the belief that person X should be doing a particular task or leading a particular body within the Church. This is a theological argument in support of the perennial desperate plea from Nomination Committee Conveners to be given more nominations from across the Church.

Then, when you begin to serve, as a new member of a Kirk Session or Presbytery, as a first-time Commissioner to the Assembly, or as a member of a committee or agency at any level of the Church's administration, speak. As my mother would say to any of us setting off to sit a school exam, 'write about what you know'. (They had to give me a good mark in my French 'O' grade, when my composition described a recent Metro journey from Place Clichy to the centre of Paris; by filling up the word-limit with a list of impeccably spelt station-names, I was spared the need to conjugate many verbs or remember many nouns. That's not what I mean here...) Speak about the experience that makes you feel this group has not properly understood you in the past: your years in rural ministry, your time as an inmate in a Scottish prison, your Masters degree in contextual New Testament exegesis... Help them to get it right.

8 Leave it all on the field

When you have shown up, spoken up, done what you were asked to do, contributed the wisdom that is uniquely yours, then for pity's sake take part in the vote. We do not record abstentions in our voting system. I think that's because when you are serving, of all things, the Body of Christ, there is surely no scope for disengaging from the work or the responsibility.

I think I'm right in believing that an abstention never has a positive effect. Let us assume that a person who abstains is not in favour of the proposal; if they liked it they would be voting 'for'. The abstainer must be at best neutral or quite possibly hostile to the motion. Let us suppose that the motion is approved, but by a very small margin; a few abstentions represent a lost opportunity to defeat the motion. Even if the motion is approved by a majority larger than the number of those who abstained, those potential votes against the motion would have given a more marginal result, which the proposing committee would be wise to remember as they take the matter forward with sensitivity to the division the debate revealed. The corollary is that if the vote goes against the motion but members abstained, the negative result may appear more marginal than it should have, thus unfortunately encouraging the Convener to come back with a modified proposal another time because the idea wasn't properly squashed flat first time round.

Is there, though, any circumstance in which it is necessary to abstain from a vote? I can think of two situations in which it might be unavoidable.

First, someone who has not been able to read or hear all the arguments on a complicated issue may be right to feel they are not qualified to make the decision. That is why reading Reports for meetings is an irreducible part of serving in any decision-making body. Someone who is called away from part of a meeting and misses substantial debate on the matter may not really be able to judge properly either; it's a matter of conscience on each occasion to know whether an abstention is the best way to respect a process or debate that you have not fully absorbed.

Second, there are rare situations in which doing nothing is not an option for the Court, and so voting against a proposal is illogical without an alternative proposal. This might be the case in a situation of a fabric emergency, where for safety reasons something has to be done and the *status quo* cannot be maintained. A common instance of 'doing nothing is not an option' recently has been the approval of Presbytery Mission Plans; the Presbytery was not at liberty to decide to do nothing because the Assembly had given them a required number of ministries to achieve, so those who disliked their committee's proposals needed to come up with an alternative proposal which they could persuade the Presbytery was better than its committee's draft Plan. If the minority tried but failed to do that, they were left with only one positive proposal available, in circumstances where a positive proposal of some kind had to be adopted. In that situation an abstention was be the resort of someone who had at some point genuinely tried and failed to promote an alternative proposal, could not in conscience approve the surviving motion as first tabled, but knew that a vote against the remaining motion would be illogical.[37] I would argue, though, that such a resort is never legitimate unless best efforts have first been made to supply a successful alternative suggestion.

9 Be a good loser

Be a good loser in the sense of being a gracious human being who does not harbour bitterness in defeat, nor personalise an impersonal debate, nor go into a sulk and stop contributing positively to the rest of the work that needs to be done.

Be a good loser like that, in the situations in which you eventually realise that you were wrong and the majority was right. If the majority includes gracious people too, you will not have to eat much humble pie, but you will be respected for an elegant about-turn and for your generous acknowledgement that the right way was chosen all along. Be a good loser like that too, though, in situations in which you remain convinced that you were right and the others really, really are wrong; as you graciously engage with the decision that has been made you might be able to mitigate some of its more dire effects, and you may be surprised to find possibilities you had not anticipated that bring something positive from an imperfect scheme.

That means being a good loser in a different sense, the kind of person your colleagues will trust to test limits, offer alternative wisdom, accept the result you didn't vote to approve, engage with the outcome and find blessings in the effects. That goes beyond a gracious or forgiving attitude, lovely though that always is to encounter in an opponent in debate; that is the hallmark of an achiever of results and not just a winner of arguments.

---

[37] I am thinking of the new united Presbytery whose Planning Committee had to be warned by the equivalent Committee of one of its constituent Presbyteries that the 'unanimous' approval of its Presbytery Mission Plan masked the disapproval of one third of its members all serving in one discrete area of its bounds; their disapproval was invisible because they had all abstained in the vote. But see subsequent paragraphs for a defence of their action.

I think St Peter was a little like that. He kept thinking he knew better, even better than Jesus, and had to be rebuked. He argued his way through the earliest years of Church history, and never fully resolved the big arguments of the day. He probably wasn't at all sure about some of the initiatives that were popping up from Paul's ministry around the wider Roman Empire. But he never sulked, never gave up, kept finding a new path when an existing one seemed to be blocked, and kept his faith to the point of being the first link in the Church's historical chain.

10. Know when to leave

St Peter didn't have the luxury of an alternative denomination to join, when the Church subsisted in such a different, emergent, varied way in its earliest days. But most Western Christians today would hold allegiance to a denomination, a polity, a self-contained religious organisation.

Dare we ask: when is it appropriate to leave completely? When is it right, as a matter of principle and not just force of circumstance, to leave one denomination and join another? The answer may vary depending on the type of Church you want to leave. When it's one like the Church of Scotland, with that distinction I made between the articles of faith we're obliged to hold and the matters on which liberty of opinion is permitted, I think there is quite a clear algorithm to apply for that kind of drastic decision.

1 If you sincerely conclude that you no longer believe something that belongs in the irreducible core of Church of Scotland beliefs, your integrity will compel you to go, so that you do not give the impression that you believe something which in fact you don't. If you are not theologically trained, please consult someone who can help you to check whether the thing that is bothering you really is something on which your belief is being compelled – you might be pleasantly surprised to find it wasn't a core item and you can stay after all! If it is one of the core bits, it

might yet be possible for you to try to generate a debate on whether that item is rightly a compulsory one; if you fail to move that needle, though, your position is untenable.

2 If you believe there is an article of your faith that ought to be in that irreducible core but is not – perhaps a moral question that your colleagues treat with liberty of opinion while you believe it should be an essential element of the Church's central beliefs – you are in a position that is the perfect mirror image of the one above, and therefore, again, your conscience probably cannot permit you to stay if you cannot successfully argue for change.

3 If you are a person of extreme integrity, you may even feel the same way about an article of faith with which you personally happen to agree, but which you do not believe should be within that compulsory substance of the faith and imposed on people you are there to serve even if you have different views on some things. Your belief in other people's liberty of opinion, though you are not yourself compromised by it, may prevent you from remaining in a flawed system.

I end with the polemical suggestion that there is no other circumstance in which leaving the institution is necessary. Losing an argument is not in itself a reason to give up, and neither is being instructed to do something you would not have chosen, or finding the Church and its assets re-shaped around you, or having to put up with people who live a life you would not feel it was right for you to live.

Isn't it always better to stay and fight to right the wrong decisions you lost, or as suggested above to make the best of them because maybe God can work through them after all? Isn't there more to lose than to gain by leaving it behind, baby with bathwater and all that?

4B CONTRIBUTION FROM GRAHAM B. USHER
ANGLICAN BISHOP OF NORWICH

Shepherds of Christ's Flock –
Episcopal Authority in the Church of England

At the consecration of a new bishop the following question is asked by the presiding Archbishop:

Will you accept the discipline of this Church, exercising authority with justice, courtesy and love, and always holding before you the example of Christ?[38]

The type of authority that a bishop is to exercise, even when in the judicial role of applying and enforcing clerical discipline, is to be patterned after Christ, knowing, as the consecration service reminds new bishops, that,

God has entrusted to your care Christ's beloved bride, his own flock, bought by the shedding of his blood on the cross.

---

[38] Common Worship (2007) *Ordination Services*. Church House Publishing, London. p. 63.

You are to govern Christ's people in truth, lead them out to proclaim the good news of the kingdom, and prepare them to stand before him when at last he comes in glory.[39]

If this, together with other questions asked, doesn't make a prospective bishop quail, or help re-boot an over-confident bishop of long service, then perhaps they should not be a bishop. Authority needs to be handled with care, with a particular concern to guard against it so easily and incipiently becoming an abuse of power. One quickly learns that you can do none of that which is asked of you as a bishop without seeking to continually be re-made holy and acceptable to God.

There is the authority that stems from the *office* one holds as a bishop, but also *personal* authority, and the authority that is *projected* onto a bishop. I will look at each of these in turn.

The bishop exercises this authority in trust. This is a trust ultimately from God and given by the Archbishop on behalf of the wider Church. It is a trust also received from the clergy and laity, indeed the wider population, of the diocese the bishop serves, who recognise that that she/he has certain skills and gifts (and vulnerabilities) that enable her/him to exercise that particular authority. The trust flows from one to the other, hopefully increasing with time.

The bishop has come from the wider body of the people, drawn from them, represents them and serves them. She/he "speaks their faith, and in so doing is the sign of their union with all other churches who profess that same faith".[40] Unlike

---

[39] Common Worship (2007) *Ordination Services*. Church House Publishing, London. p. 63.

[40] Halliburton, J. (1987) *The Authority of a Bishop*. SPCK, London. p. 51.

a contract, this relationship is covenantal, and why in England the bishop, as an office holder, receives the Archbishop's Charge, an initial list of priorities to direct their ministry, drawn up in consultation with the Crown Nomination Commission who recommended their appointment to the Sovereign. Those who are suffragan or assistant bishops receive delegated authority from their diocesan bishop, mostly to fulfil all episcopal functions, but without the ability to delegate!

The authority within which bishops act comes from Measures (laws which relate to the administration and organisation of the Church of England with the same force and effect as Acts of Parliament), Canons and guidance, itself stemming from how the Church approaches discernment, debate, dialogue, agreement, disagreement, decision making and reception of those decisions. Thus, decisions are always made within a framework of authority.

An example is how a bishop exercises their authority in making appointments within the diocese. There may be appointments to local trusts or educational foundations which require a representative of the bishop. Care will be needed to appoint people with the desired skills and to foster a trust that the individual will exercise that responsibility wisely and diligently so that the bishop maintains enough oversight but without being drawn into operational matters. Likewise, with the work and ministry of diocesan officers and the bishop's senior clergy colleagues.

When making appointments to parishes, a bishop must work within the framework of various measures and policy guidance, such as the Mission and Pastoral Measure, the patronage system and Common Tenure. The appointment of clergy is a complicated process including strategic resource planning involving various committees of the diocese, and formal consultation with Parochial Church Councils (PCCs), patrons of the living (who exercise a historic right of presenting a potential incumbent to the bishop) and others. Thus, whilst appointments are made by the bishop and are under her/his authority, they are not made at the bishop's unfettered discretion. This is a much more complex process than is required in a secular context, with the added complexity of differing traditions of churchmanship which may lead to conflicts of interest.

An example of the latter may be the capacity of PCC's to pass a resolution seeking extended episcopal oversight; or the potential differences of approach which may follow an introduction this autumn of *Prayers of Love and Faith* (including prayers of blessing after a same sex marriage), which risks further undermining episcopal authority as people will be free to exercise their own conscience.

Congregations and the wider public often have the impression that a bishop is a figure of authority, but the practical capacity to manage a cleric once they have been appointed is challenging. It relies almost entirely on goodwill, moral encouragement, and an appeal to their vocation, since a bishop has few levers available to 'manage' office holders, other than the Clergy Discipline Measure and the Common Tenure capability process. A bishop can't dismiss an incumbent from office apart from these procedures, or other more obscure and difficult procedures, such as the Incumbents (Vacation of Benefices) Measure. Like the capability procedure, hardly anyone uses these procedures because they are so lengthy and cumbersome, resulting in some clergy pushing boundaries of behaviour quite a long way without any real risk of sanction. As clergy are 'office holders', affording them various protections, it is very difficult for a bishop to fire a priest unless there is a serious disciplinary issue resulting in a penalty of removal from office either by consent or imposed by a Tribunal.

Such clergy seem to have forgotten that at their ordination and at each move of ministry requiring a new licence, together with licensed lay ministers, they swear an oath of canonical obedience to the bishop:

I, A B, do swear by Almighty God that I will pay true and canonical obedience to the Bishop of C and his/her successors in all things lawful and honest: so help me God.[41]

There has been much debate about this oath, including its original meaning, as the words are from an ancient, pre-Reformation oath (though the earliest known example in print, in the original Latin, dates from 1713) when they would have been part of obedience in a feudal society.

The oath is made to an individual person, but is not attached to that person but to the office of the diocesan bishop, and neither is it dependent on the individual beliefs or virtues of that bishop as it points to being loyal to the historic and corporate teaching of the Church of England. Above all, the oath is seeking good relationships and a reminder that we are all accountable, ministering under authority, ultimately to answer before God for that which was entrusted to us.

What constitutes 'lawful' and 'honest' has long been debated. This was largely settled by the Judicial Committee of the Privy Council in its 1863 judgement *Long vs Bishop of Cape Town*: "the oath of canonical obedience does not mean that every clergyman will obey all the commands of the bishop against which there is no law, but that he will obey all such commands as the bishop by law

---

[41] Common Worship (2007) *Ordination Services*. Church House Publishing, London. p. 6.

is authorised to impose".[42] At heart, the oath's mention of things lawful (ie the Canons), made before a bishop under the same rules[43], is both personal and institutional, and a reminder that:

> Without some practical rules there would be chaos and confusion. The canons help us to provide structure and order, to avoid dissensions in the Church, and to foster mission. They are not intended as unnecessarily restrictive but as a set of parameters to help build healthy congregations and relationships of mutual, covenantal loyalty and trust.[44]

The authority of the bishop is most publicly visible when they are president of their Diocesan Synod and chair of their Bishop's Council. These roles of the bishop, as representative of their local church on provincial synod or ecumenical council, have a history far back into antiquity. Both are arenas where bishops need to listen more than speak. They can also be places where the moral leadership of the bishop can move things forward in a positive way, though sometimes, due to an unhealthy deference culture, members of Synods and Councils can feel inhibited from saying what they really think.

A foolish bishop will arrive in a diocese with their own plan to be put into action. Instead, what is needed is attentive watching, the seeking of wisdom from people across the diocese (especially under-represented and marginalised groups) and attending prayerfully to God's call alongside the whole people

---

[42] The Faith and Order Commission of the Church of England (2022) *To Proclaim Afresh: Declaration and Oaths for Church of England Ministers.* Church House Publishing, London. p. 25.

[43] Canon C14, Of the Oaths of Obedience

[44] The Faith and Order Commission of the Church of England (2022) *To Proclaim Afresh: Declaration and Oaths for Church of England Ministers.* Church House Publishing, London. pp. 24-25.

of God. From this will hopefully emerge a clear vision for bishop, clergy and people in Synod (which literally means 'people on the way') and their life together in the diocese. The bishop will have an eye to represent the national and universal Church to the local Church, and *vice versa* in this process. When the bishop can articulate a collective vision, and engender even a modicum of goodwill, there can be much energy, though this still requires patience in enabling people to become accustomed to new ideas and then refocussing their energies appropriately. However, there is also the check and balance that the Synod could vote down all of the bishop's proposals, though hopefully consultation, attentive listening and the wisdom of senior colleagues will have honed and shaped ideas to encompass a larger tent.

What is at play here is the bishop exercising less of their authority of office and more their personal authority. That authority comes from the bishop's engagement with scripture, tradition and reason, as well as their conscience and experience. Avis helpfully reminds us that "personal qualities to which authority accrues are holiness, prayerfulness, humility, dedication, self-sacrifice, compassion"[45]. If rooted in these virtues, this type of personal episcopal authority encourages and enables people to see value in the bishop's way of thinking and the direction of travel. This is how culture change happens, for good or ill.

As with many other Churches and institutions, the Church of England has had to face up to the sin and criminality of child sexual abuse in its past and present. Measures have been passed, policy guidance issued, and expert safeguarding staff recruited to enable the Church to become as safe as possible.

---

[45] Avis, P. (2015) *Becoming a Bishop: A Theological Handbook of Episcopal Ministry*. Bloomsbury T&T Clark, London. p. 44.

However, whilst I can exercise the authority of my office in demanding certain actions, it is my personal authority, committed to safeguarding and learning from survivors, and modelling these behaviours, that is able to make the biggest difference with culture, and thus change hearts and minds so that safeguarding is everyone's responsibility, rooted in what we believe as Christians, and not a box ticking hurdle.

A bishop can hold authority within the context of where they minister and the media carry stories about bishops who speak out nationally, especially if they disagree with the policies of the Government of the day. In many ways I am saying much the same things as I did as a parish priest, but my words as a bishop seem to be listened to more, and certainly, both positively and negatively, the media pays more attention, much to the envy of some ecumenical colleagues. This public square ministry is a privilege and not a right. It is changing. Whilst in the past the Church could speak with some authority about virtually any social or moral issue, that has been eroded in a culture where there is a strong emphasis on individual determination of standards and what is right or appropriate, but also because the Church and its leaders have been found to be hypocritical or wanting. The scaffolding is still there, but it can often appear to be around a house needing to get itself in order about such things as safeguarding, power, sexuality and the role of woman.

Finally, the authority of projection is one that needs careful attention. Bishops have their devotees and their despisers, though the Church would be better without both and would definitely be a happier place! Avis comments that "to the world at large, to those Christians who have never met them in the flesh, bishops (and even more, archbishops) are hardly real people: they are projections, figments, symbols, ciphers".⁴⁶ I would add: to many people we are an irrelevance. Whilst uncritical devotion and cringing acceptance of authority is deeply unhealthy, even dangerous, it is equally concerning that some clergy and laity feel within their rights to disregard that authority altogether. Criticism of bishops seems fair game, especially on Anglican twitter, quite often hidden behind pseudonyms, and is aimed disproportionately at bishops who are women. There are many situations where we cannot give a balanced view due to confidentiality and instead our leadership has to be one of non-anxious presence. Another example is the priest who sees you as their 'father in God' and will come and dump their problems at your door. This dependence or projected behaviour needs to be gently challenged and self-confidence rebuilt, so that there can be a pastoral conversation that helps them pick up the pieces, have agency and move forward. All of these situations take up a disproportionate amount of a bishop's time and energy!

Thus, authority as experienced by a bishop in the Church of England is personal, collegial and communal, and there should always be alertness to the fact that no bishop can "bear the weight of this calling in [their] own strength, but only by the grace and power of God".⁴⁷

---

⁴⁶ Avis, P. (2015) *Becoming a Bishop: A Theological Handbook of Episcopal Ministry*. Bloomsbury T&T Clark, London. p. 41.
⁴⁷ Common Worship (2007) *Ordination Services*. Church House Publishing, London. p. 63.

4C POWER IN THE CONGREGATION
From *Speaking from the Heart*

If ever there existed a social organism that would repay psychological or systems-theory scrutiny, it would be a good-sized Church of Scotland congregation. For a body called to be a single spiritual entity and designed to achieve laudable tasks, a congregation often seems rather to be a fascinating web of relationships and dynamics, and some of them can seem competitive and stressful.

The human yearning for control

Human insecurity is one of the fundamental problems we spend our lives trying to overcome. It seems to be part of our original condition, as if part of the punishment for that distant ancestral horror that Christians tell and re-tell because it comforts us as we try to make sense of the ultimate inadequacy of even the best of us. The sinister suspicion we each have that we live dangerously close to a loss of control over our circumstances – at any moment accident, bereavement, someone else's terrible mistake or our own overwhelming temptation could drag us into a most terrifying new existence – makes us maximise the comfort and confidence we have in our present surroundings, because then we feel less vulnerable.

Any human institution provides a finite environment which provides the same anxieties and needs, and in which we play out the strategies of coping with uncertainty and weakness. An organisation has a membership, a structure, a way of operating, a way of regulating the routine and non-routine events in its corporate life. An organisation has roles for people, things for them to achieve; it has, in other words, ways for a person to be someone, something. Each human institution, to some varying extent, provides a setting for human beings to enact those relationships of power and control which meet such a visceral need in each poor one of us.

The Church paints that environment, those opportunities, its structures and activities, in very bright colours indeed. The Church offers to engage with people deep below most of their outer layers of confidence, cheerfulness and coping, and reaches in to the places where we keep our fears tucked away. The Church announces challenges to people that question those very parts of them, difficult challenges in the areas of principle, conduct, relationships, morality, spirituality. The Church appears to promise that the most fragile and unattractive characters of our human community will have an equal place and dignity amongst us. The Church, obeying its very purpose and mandate, sets itself up as the place above all others where the dynamics of personal power will be virtually uncontainable.

Church and the need for control

When a new minister arrives in a congregation, makes promises at his[48] induction service and wakes up the next morning in his unfamiliar new manse, he is aware that he faces the now-famous quartet: known knowns, unknown knowns, known unknowns and unknown unknowns. The known knowns include the information he has been given, the research on the area he has been able to do, and the standard challenges and needs of every parish that will come as no surprise therefore in this one. The unknown knowns include his own ministerial formation and education, the mental and spiritual equipment that will sustain him without his always realising it, and the people he has not met but whose fears and griefs he already understands. The unknown unknowns await him behind closed doors in the parish, in the unexpected requests that will make him laugh or make him quake, in the achievements he will one day be proud of (but better to be in ignorance of them meantime).

The dynamics of power and fear, mixed up in so many of the people who are welcoming him to their congregation, provide one of the principal 'known unknowns' to the minister. He could see the people sitting in the pews at the induction service, but he has scarcely begun to figure out the wiring that really connects them. Some of it will be easy to uncover: who is related to whom by blood, marriage, friendship or intimacy. Some of it will be explicit: who engage with each other in recognised congregational groups, who share tasks. And the most important parts of it can only be discovered over a longer time spent there: where is trust, where is mistrust, who hogs tasks and who covets them, who has influence, who is marked for life by disappointment, what never works smoothly because the wrong

---

[48] Pronouns are used arbitrarily throughout this collection!

combination of people collide every time. The wise minister knows all of these are there to be found, while the foolish one treats the congregation as if no-one is so human.

Task, status and ownership

If this network of connections and collisions of people is a kind of economy, then its currencies are task and status. This fallen human feels that this week she has a contribution to make because the flowers in the vestibule this Sunday will be ones she has put there and arranged. That fallen human has sat in the tenor section of the choir for forty years now, and is rightly conscious of the wonderful difference his voice has made to the praise of God in that place, and it is a natural part of how he thinks of himself and his worth. And this other fallen human looks at the pointing round the vestry window, and properly takes quiet satisfaction from her convenership of the property task group that decided to have that work done. And that fallen human over there is the Ordained Local Minister, and probably could not cope very well if she were not.

Sometimes, though, the task or the status becomes the kind of currency that people covet too much, and there develops a possessiveness, a territorial defensiveness, that spoils how people manage with each other. The finance convener stops consulting the task group, and regards them as thoroughly ungrateful when they challenge the actions she has taken without their authority. The Session Clerk adjusts the minutes of the meeting to reflect what really ought to have been decided. The soprano whose voice has long since failed sits relentlessly in the front row of the choir and wordlessly defies the choirmaster to rescue the quality of the music by removing her. The minister changes the familiar practice of long years so fast that gentle souls are frightened to the core and lose any sense of religious security they ever knew. Each one of them, probably, is acting out of their own fears and inadequacies.

The organist, and others[49]

The relationship of minister and organist is sometimes used to illustrate the problems. Each of them has their area of training and speciality, but each of them has been around the Church long enough to know quite a bit about the other's role and task. The organist often has a strong personal faith, and therefore has opinions about the whole service and not just its music; while the minister may happen to be musical enough to be able to think critically about the musical life of the worshipping community. They are regularly engaged together in a task with overlapping elements, trying to integrate what each can bring into a flowing sequence that will affect and effect the worship of themselves and others. They are constantly required to walk onto each other's territory, exchange the currency of their responsibilities, meet – and more than meet – each other and survive the meeting. Their relationship requires a level of trust and mutual respect that exists far more often than it is absent; and where it exists perhaps a small miracle must have happened every time.

An example as easy to understand as that one tells us that we must be capable of understanding how all sorts of people, encountering each other in the work of congregational life, may have the same difficulty. So it is not that organists are peculiarly unreasonable people, nor that ministers expect the worst from them and by expecting it get it. You can see the collision approaching in slow motion at the moment that a very musical minister arrives in a town not quite big enough for both of them;

---

[49] This essay was written many years ago, and does not describe any individual.

but you can see it too when a long-served fabric convener spots the arrival of an imaginative young architect in the midst of the congregation. For that matter, you can see the stress increase when the new minister announces she does not like flower vases on the communion table, where they have been since the beadle's mother who died last month first started putting them there in the very vases she gifted just after her wedding in 1965. You can see the anxiety in the eyes of the Deacons' Court clerk who realises in horror that the new Session Clerk is doing the Session minutes on a computer, and someone soon is surely going to want all minutes done the same way, far outside his area of competence.

It can happen to anyone; their insecurities are jolted, even in the very institution where they thought they should have safe space made for them, and sometimes, sadly, they do something to try to put right by force (because nothing else will work) what is making them feel so threatened.

Bullying

According to the law of the Church " "Bullying" shall mean a course of conduct (i.e. conduct which occurs on at least two occasions) amounting to offensive, threatening, abusive, malicious, intimidating or insulting behaviour that may be an abuse or misuse of power, position or knowledge through means that undermine, humiliate, denigrate or injure the person concerned and which is behaviour occurring in circumstances where it would appear to a reasonable individual that it would amount to bullying of that person." [Act 1, 2019 s.1(7)]

In every human institution, in every period of history, personal interaction suffers from the mildest versions of that human sin, so mild that most of the time people do not resort to legal process, so mild that most of the time people would not use the lexicon of 'bullying' language to describe it. In fact the legal use of it tends to be confined to two sorts of very unusual circumstances: first, when the alleged bully is thought to have dishonourable motives for their activity; and, second, when the bully is regarded as exercising great strength or authority that must be curbed. While that may be true, it is important for ministers and other leaders to grasp that sometimes manipulation has everything to do with weakness not strength, and everything to do with wanting to achieve perfectly good ends not evil ones.

When behaviour does not seem to warrant the use of an emotive word like 'bullying', it is all too easy to underestimate it. Low-level manipulation, skilful political operating, tactical 'dealing' in the commodities of status, task and respect; these run through congregational life, often amongst the sweetest, most dedicated, wisest and kindest of people, all trying to do the right thing and even for the right reasons. Spotting it is three-quarters of the battle in surviving it.

Strength and weakness

Weakness is a terribly underestimated threat in church life. It marks not only the causes and motivations for bad behaviour, but it characterises the very conduct itself in ways that some ministers and office-bearers never seem to recognise, fascinating ways that explain why the worshipping community is always such a complicated social organism.

Strength is rarely the initial cause when one person uses distress or compulsion to bend another to his aims. If this individual were in a position of strength, with the better argument or the church's regulation or the majority of the Kirk Session on his side, there would be no need to waste bullying behaviour (and therefore reputation) on the situation, as the debate would be won before it had begun. Rather, it is the very insecure person, fearing their own fragility, who jumps in despair over the line between acceptable and unacceptable personal dynamics, doing whatever it takes to protect something they fear losing.

When it comes to method, weakness is used as often as strength in the setting of the Church (where the weak are supposed to be so particularly welcome). In a show of his strength, the praise band leader who is defeated in a passionate Session debate tonight may be suddenly and mysteriously unavailable for next week's family service, wrecking a special occasion most effectively. In a show of her strength, the offended elder whose grand-daughter's baptism the minister was unable to agree to do may mobilise her friends on the Board to vote against the minister's pet buildings plan. In a gesture of utter weakness, though, the disappointed Sunday School teacher may burst uncontrollably into tears upon discovering that she's due to take the difficult P7 boys, and the terrified Superintendent opts for the easy life by re-shuffling the staff instead. In an apparent expression of weakness, a certain kind of church worker will adopt full martyr mode, doing jobs others admire them for doing, always with an air of selfless suffering, and milking the resulting sympathy for all its worth when times are hard.

Those who have worked out the possibilities of weakness as a lever might as well discover here in this book that the generation of Church of Scotland ministers who endured their Church Law training at the hands of this author has been taught to identify and disarm the pinnacle of that tactic, the use of threatened resignation. One of the greatest fears of many ministers is the difficulty of recruiting people into certain posts (treasurer, safeguarding co-ordinator, property convener, and the like).

Those who undertake those roles benefit from a background atmosphere of relieved gratitude, because by their presence they keep the spectre of an unfillable vacancy at bay. The biggest lever they have in any dispute – a dispute that may have nothing whatever to do with that job – is the threat that they will resign, and leave the minister, Session Clerk or other adversary with a nightmare of a hole.

I have always advised ministers to adopt a strategy that will cost short-term pain for a long-term prize worth the price. Always, always accept resignations, genuine or tactical. Never, ever reverse the decision. Accept them quickly, courteously, regretfully even, but unwaveringly. Do the job yourself for a time, if that's what it takes (not treasurer, for legal reasons, but otherwise crack on if you must). If it happens a second time, the second person probably failed to understand what was happening, and it really, really will not happen a third time. Or perhaps it will, but it won't be for purposes of manipulation; it will be the manipulators giving up and going away.

Well-intentioned bullies

Another tendency of the fallen human condition is to imagine that one must be morally superior to one's rivals in an argument. Just as God must be on my side when my country is at war, so the most intense disagreements in congregational life can blind the combatants into thinking there is a battle of good and evil intentions taking place, and no-one ever believes he is on the 'wrong' side. Those outside the struggle can see both points of view with an impartial eye: Presbytery and Assembly Clerks trying to give procedural advice, staff members in the Faith Nurture Forum and elsewhere, ministers who might be lucky enough not to be embroiled in the argument, people in unconnected congregations, all can see the good but incompatible visions that divide people to the point of bitterness.

The fact that someone is indulging in improper behaviour to secure their own interests is no evidence that their interests are bad ones. The most sincerely-held beliefs can result in the most unfair behaviour. The most profoundly-sensed vocation can make people stop at nothing to secure a role of leadership. An unshakable belief about our faith's moral teachings can lead to hurtful opposition to another person's choices in life. The trouble is, it would be so much neater and easier, and so much more satisfying, if one's opponents could be guaranteed to be the bad guys. Yet even those whose bad judgement takes my breath away are doing their best for the Church that is theirs as much as mine, and for the God of both of us.

Disarming with trust

Those who are called to the highest tasks of leadership in the Church community have the task of preventing and removing the games of power they find around them. First and foremost they will long to avoid being players in those games themselves, but their own tasks and status conspire to place them directly in that harm's way from many directions.

Those who succeed best of all, so much so that they manage to continue to love their people and even to be loved in return, often include those who practise the extraordinary and noble discipline of attributing the best of motivations to everyone they encounter. Such a minister, who disagrees with a member on the most far-reaching question of moral principle or contends with a colleague over an irksome detail of practice, nevertheless has it in her to treat the other as having a perfectly legitimate point of view and the right for it to be heard and weighed with respect. Friendship and love are bigger there than the anxieties that produced the disagreement. That minister, in fact, is probably more secure than most, and less driven by deep fragility within her own spirit.

How different the General Assembly or Presbytery would be if everyone there treated everyone else as being good and godly, even when believing their arguments to be wrong. How disarming of the few who are just too ruthless, when they are not given the satisfaction of an asymmetric fight against someone they can bend or compel.

Consider the awful responsibility of co-ordinating the appraisal and adjustment of parish resources, as everyone has been doing in the Planning process already described. There now is a role and a task that is rarely coveted in any Presbytery. There is a convener who does not relish his status, and few struggle to keep the job. There is someone with an infinite capacity to bring out the worst and most paranoid feelings in those he encounters in his work.

The hearts of members of the Church's judicial bodies, hearing appeals in adjustment cases, inevitably sink as the papers and pleadings arrive, revealing yet another argument by congregational members who have persuaded themselves that their Presbytery is out to get them, has it in for them, has always been trying to do them down, is taking wicked pleasure in closing them... and the reader will know of other familiar complaints. Those sitting in the appeal are themselves members of other Presbyteries, and know that no-one takes pleasure in the loss of a congregation, and know that it is with the heaviest of hearts that their committees find ways to meet the challenge of shrinking financial resources throughout Scotland, and know how painful it all is for sensitive, decent ministers and elders to have to make these things happen. If the complainers had attributed more kindly motives to their Presbytery's representatives, they would be working with them to make the best of their circumstances, not heading towards the shock of being put out of their misery by the system.

The Golden Rule

There is a secret formula for all of this grief and tension. It is a formula as old as the Gospel that expresses it: do to others as you would have them do to you. Perhaps congregational life, those few hours in the week when that human machine comes together to do its thing, perhaps that is a place just small enough for the Golden Rule to work. At every turning-point of discussion, at every moment of allocation of status or task, in every difficult encounter, things are turned upside down for good when one of the parties thinks into the place and need and point of view of the other, and asks what that person expects of him in exactly that moment. In our cinematic age, we can imagine turning the camera round to film each scene over the shoulder of the other person, our own faces being the focus of the drama, our own choices being the substance of the plot. Entering the other person's needs, suspicions and fears breaks through to him more than any other approach.

What, for instance, would happen if every member of every church choir in Scotland recorded their own voice, singing along to a CD of hymns, and listened to it? What would happen if each of them pretended to be the local choirmaster, and asked 'Would we be better off if the choir did not include this voice?'. And what would happen if those who realised it was time for them to go invented an elegant excuse for leaving ('I'm giving so-and-so a lift to church, so can't manage rehearsals before the service any more', or similar), so that the choirmaster would not be compelled to fib 'but you have a lovely voice' and find both of them back where they started?

What would happen if the members of large and wealthy congregations resisted running the old argument 'you can't close us, we are financially self-sustaining' when the Presbytery was talking about uniting their 300 members with a congregation of 400 members lying 250 yards away, into their building that seats 800? What would happen if their Kirk Session took a few hours to go and visit the massively aid-receiving congregation of 50, which just happened to have a much higher per capita giving than theirs and lay 25 miles from the next church building of any kind, and thought a bit about where the Presbytery needs to close a church?

What would happen if the elder who has read the lesson at the Watchnight Service for the last twenty years let go a little and tried to get inside the thinking of the Bible Class leader, who would love to ask one of her 12-year-olds to do that reading and have an experience of worship that could inspire him for a lifetime? Better still, what would happen if that elder went one step further and congratulated the child on the reading, whether it was done well or badly?

Faith is ennobled and strengthened every week in parishes across the Church of Scotland, whenever the upside-downness of the Gospel gets the better of people.

5 FROM SCAPEGOAT TO SHIBBOLETH

Just after the General Assembly of 2021, which sent down under the Barrier Act the Overture that was to become the Church's legislation enabling the conduct of same-sex weddings, I published this part-theological, part-personal piece of writing in the private Facebook group 'Affirmation Scotland'. From the perspective of one side of the protracted sexuality debate, I tried to look with compassion and through a theological lens at those with whom I disagreed, and to acknowledge how their pain must have unfolded.

I present it in this new collection of essays as a stark example of everything I've wrestled with in the foregoing pages. It is an illustration of attempts at corporate discernment, institutional-level theologising, brave leadership, and less brave disengagement by some of those with things to fear. Try, if you possibly can, to read it as a treatment of Church process, putting aside the prejudice you bring to the substance of the debate.

What's unique about the sexuality debate?

What's unique about the sexuality debate compared with eg women's ordination? Were not those two things examples of the same stand-off between the same ecclesiastical tribes, just living a generation apart in the Church of Scotland? Surely both triggered visceral reactions, caused existential hurt to individuals as well as to the national institution, changed the way the Church is seen by its surrounding culture. Both were applications of a more generic debate about the Bible, were about the admission of whole categories of people to office within the Church, were transformative of theological balance and character across the country.

No; they were not the same at all. In two ways (or so it feels to a woman who has thrived in ministry while trapped in the closet by the sexuality debate for almost a whole professional lifetime), this is a completely different issue.

Firstly, had I been an adult in the 1960s, no-one would have told me that I ought not to express my identity as a woman; only that I could not be ordained to ministry as one. The sexuality debate, however, is framed the other way round; those who take the traditionalist position allow me to be a minister, and then constrain my expression of my personal identity. The first frustrates my vocation, but the second frustrates my personhood.

Secondly, without going into the emotional debate about gender and sex identity involving JK Rowling and others, no-one criticises me for being a woman as if it has been a *choice*, a moral *decision*, a reprehensibly deliberate *act*. The language of gay 'lifestyle', on the other hand, still persists in some quarters, despite the fact that no sane Church member would have *chosen* that identity (the implication of the word 'lifestyle'), if they could - somehow - choose another while such resistance and exclusion was widespread in the faith community.

This, then, is a debate that is distinctive, more than just a new expression of the battles of a previous generation. And for that reason, I think we need to look with immense compassion at the effect it has had on those most hurt by it.

When did the balance shift?

The Church seems to have moved from a majority-traditional to a majority-affirming position, but I'm not sure quite when the scales tipped. You might arbitrarily pick the General Assembly of 2015 when it passed Act I[50], which *explicitly* enables Kirk Sessions of vacant congregations to declare those in same-sex marriages and civil partnerships eligible to apply for their charge, thereby *implicitly* removing the fear of disciplinary action from any gay or lesbian minister or would-be minister. (The jury remains out on trans, intersex and other queer categories.)

But to pick that date is to mistake the symbolic for the substantive. The balance of opinion had shifted somewhere before that, surely, to enable that seismic event to happen.

You might be tempted to say it shifted much earlier, before the Assembly of 1992, where an attempt to have Rev Margaret Forrester disciplined for her affirmative actions in relation to a same-sex couple failed. Perhaps a majority of that Assembly thought she had done the right thing. More likely only a minority agreed with her, but a significant number thought it was a matter for her conscience and supported her right to do something with which they individually disagreed, or were simply not convinced her actions should have triggered disciplinary action. I don't think it quite proves anything.

I think that for many years between 1992 and 2015 the Church, as a collection of people each with their own opinions, just didn't know what 'it' thought. There were people who were clear they agreed with one side of the argument. There were people who were equally clear they agreed with the other. And there were lots of people who, in that circular way our Church has, were waiting for clear guidance on what their opinion was, so that they could then lend their weight to one or other side, and the guidance took

---

[50] 2015 Act I: Ministers and Deacons in Civil Partnerships and Same-Sex Marriages

a long time to become clear enough. And that curious third group – opinion-formers unable to do their job until their opinion was formed by someone else – was too large to allow any of us to know where the majority truly lay. It gave us a long and difficult wait.

One close observer of that time observes that society too was shifting, away from being shocked by the idea of gay ministers, towards being shocked at the way they were treated – or maybe just increasingly away from caring much what the Church thought about anything much. Fair point.

The Scapegoat

When those who believed that homosexuality was somehow wrong (as a disordered *state*, or a sinful *choice*) still were (or at least thought that they were) the majority, some of us who held the minority view recognised what René Girard described in *The Scapegoat*[51] and believed that gay and gay-supporting ministers and members were, collectively, the scapegoat of the generation of the 1990s and 2000s.

Girard talked[52] about the choosing by an insecure majority of a topic or object of condemnation that would strengthen that majority's sense of identity together through their common revulsion. The ejection of that object of hatred as scapegoat was meant to seal the position of that power-group. That happens in many places and there is nothing *necessarily* evil about it. The platoon of soldiers who have endured together a horror so deep they can never properly convey it to anyone else will find strength and meaning within that same group and talking about that danger, demonising their enemies, for ever. A congregation may be more tightly bound in love for one another and suspicious of outside authority when it feels its future is under threat by the

---

[51] René Girard, *The Scapegoat*, Baltimore: Johns Hopkins University Press 1986
[52] James Alison helpfully articulates this theory in *Faith Beyond Resentment: Fragments Catholic and Gay*, London: DLT 2002

larger institution. There is, in other words, nothing necessarily evil about the way people act out when they are terrified by their own lack of security. It is the naming of what is abhorrent that achieves the empowering result.

Girard goes on, quite mesmerisingly, to talk about the unexpected effect of Christ being made the scapegoat of all scapegoats, but of course refusing to stay exiled or destroyed, and turning that process to utterly different effect, achieving a very different sort of transformation of individual and community. I don't need that part of his argument to make mine here; but commend his whole thesis for those who want to take this argument further.

Enough for me to suggest that the sexuality question presented itself at just the right time, when the Church was feeling threatened as a shrinking institution in a culture of post-modern mind-shifts, for its minority to serve as obvious candidates for a kind of group scapegoat. Thoughtful voices from that former majority position have said they regretted that this was the issue that happened to present itself and be seized on in this way. It would have been better to argue about something more general and (for them) more important; it would have been better, frankly, to name the real, bigger divisive issue which was and remains the authority and interpretation of the Bible.

But the scapegoating didn't quite happen; it didn't quite work. It didn't quite happen because the LGBTQ+ membership of the Church either left the institution or remained in the closet. A scapegoat is not a scapegoat if it is invisible.[53] A few 'out' gay ministers and others in our Church have had to bear a very heavy load; and many of us feel quite ashamed to have left them to do so

---

[53] The same wise commentator who made the earlier point about social attitudes also points out that it was the restraint, the dignity, the lack of stridency in the behaviour of those in the eye of the storm – in the General Assembly and elsewhere – that would have made their victimisation and scapegoating a mistaken move by those on the other side of the argument. Affirmation Scotland certainly tried to provide that kind of moderation.

alone. But somehow they clung on, enough of them with enough grit and courage, and just would not allow the load to be put on their backs and the villagers to drive them out into the wilderness.

And somewhere in those awful years of distrust and existential worry for so many, that tipping-point was reached, who knows exactly when. And then the majority and minority parties swapped places, without realising it at the time. After 2015, the balance began to tip in favour of what was known as the 'affirming' position. Fears shrank; closet doors opened a crack to allow all sorts of people in the Church to peep out; nervous conversations began to be held. And so, of course, despair began to be located on the other side of the argument from before.

Say 'shibboleth'[54]

This useful little story, from part of the Bible not otherwise much used in preaching, sees the sorry remnants of the Ephraimite army fleeing the battle they had lost to the Gileadites and trying to escape over the fords of the Jordan by pretending to be someone else. The victorious Gileadite soldiers challenged any they found there to say the word 'shibboleth', containing the 'sh' sound those foreigners could not pronounce; and those who failed the test were for the chop.

In the popular application of the story, the word shibboleth is used to denote an entrance test, a means of access into a restricted, privileged community. And that, it seems to me, is how it operates today in the community of those 'traditionalist' Christians, now the minority in our Church, who used to be the majority.

To change your opinion on the gay issue requires you to change your opinion on how you handle Biblical interpretation. To decide that the six or seven 'killer proof texts' on homosexuality are no longer insurmountable requires you to

---

[54] Judges 12:1-6

interpret them differently, or apply a slightly different hermeneutical framework, or depart altogether from a prooftexting strategy. And if you do that for those verses, you have no reason any more not to do it for other ones on all sorts of issues. Your interpretive edifice has suddenly crumbled; and you are no longer quite the conservative evangelical you once seemed to be to those who prized that in you. A constant stream of autobiographies tells the story again and again of seeing that different light, and what an emotional and unpleasant journey it is for so many.[55]

The part of the Church that still thinks in what I would call the old way is significant but shrinking. It is shrinking for two reasons. One is that some of its number left the Church after the 2015 General Assembly. (Wasn't it confusing, when a 'departing congregation' sometimes meant what it means in Act I 2015 ie departing from the traditional position, but sometimes it meant literally departing from the denomination ie adhering so fiercely to the traditional position that they didn't feel they could remain with the rest of us? It was not easy to explain this to congregations!) The other reason that constituency is shrinking is that many within it are changing their minds, and – if my argument above is right – changing profoundly as a result.

Who is left there, and how do they know whom to trust? They know it by setting an unspoken but unmistakeable test. Hostility to the Assembly's new position on this issue is that shibboleth of the conservative end of the Church, that test of continuing conservative orthodoxy, not just on this but on all things. And I completely understand that, and don't blame them. It must be terrifying.

The result is that people who have perfectly normal, predictable, liberal attitudes to past controversies (like women's ordination or ecumenical engagement) maintain breathtaking

---

[55] A particularly difficult read in this genre is Megan Phelps-Roper's *Unfollow:: A Memoir of Loving and Leaving Westboro Baptist Church*, Ardsley NY: Riverrun 2019

opposition to the 'departure' of their congregations, ie to the decision of their Kirk Session in a vacancy to instruct the Nominating Committee to consider all applicants and not preclude any in same-sex marriages. It's astonishing to the outside observer – as if you were to discover your child's headteacher was a proponent of compulsory right-handedness.[56] But it's unavoidable; it's their proof of identity, their shibboleth.

Conclusion

The true definition of liberalism is not moderation of theology, or a particular hermeneutical preference in Biblical studies, far less an identifiable style and content of services of worship. Ecclesiastical liberalism is one thing only: the irreducible belief in the right of one's theological opponents to co-exist within your ecclesial community at denominational level. (That's the approach I was crediting to the General Assembly's majority when I declined above to date the tipping-point of this debate to the Forrester controversy of 1992.)

Our Church of Scotland has a fragile minority clinging with a desperate grip to their place in the institution they dearly love, but its identity has reversed over the last ten years. No longer is it the largely invisible constituency of those of us whose very hearts were not sure of a welcome if we spoke our own truth. Now it is the community of those whose hearts were broken by the actions of the General Assembly of 2015. They are hanging grimly on to their membership of our Church, even as they have deep doubts about the legitimacy of mine.

---

[56] Though I have argued earlier that the sexuality debate is in some ways unique, it can be useful to substitute a less emotive ground of discrimination to gain a calmer perspective. I tried to do this with left-handedness, in *Speaking from the Heart*. Like homosexual orientation, left-handedness has in the past been treated as something that could be overcome by willpower and education, so I hope it is was a useful analogy to make a thinly-veiled point more than a decade ago.

As time passes, more and more Kirk Sessions will decide to 'depart' in the sense of taking the liberalising step, and more and more scared LGBTQ+ members (and especially clergy) will come out publicly and reveal the rainbow reality of our institution. If we are truly liberals, however, our calling will be to understand, respect, make room for and love the broken-hearted who so struggle to understand why *we* are here, who so struggle – I guess – to be confident that *they* are still here too.

6 SERMON PREACHED AT THE INDUCTION OF A MINISTER

In every induction service there is one moment that all the other ministers present listen for carefully; and it's the 'they are' moment. They know what I'm talking about! The vows [...] will take this evening, and which she has taken before most recently when she began her ministry in [...], all take the form of questions to which the answer is 'I do': do you believe x, do you promise y, do you concur with z? But hidden in the bunch is one that has the answer 'they are'; and we all listen out for it and remember the moments we stood there concentrating on the one with the different answer so we wouldn't get it wrong!

And that vow is one of the most splendid snippets of prose in our Presbyterian tradition: *Are not zeal for the glory of God, love to the Lord Jesus Christ, and a desire for the salvation of all, so far as you know your own heart, your great motives and chief inducements to enter into this Ministry?* **They are.** That is a magnificent little jewel in our ordinal book: it has elegance of construction, timelessness of language, incision into the very soul of the person making the response, and a depth of theology I'm sure we rarely allow ourselves to hear.

If [...] fulfils that vow as minister of [...], we will notice, everybody will notice.

Zeal for the glory of God... what a thing to have driving you, zeal for the glory of God! In a polite society where we try not to offend people, we probably avoid having very much zeal about anything. No-one likes a zealot. But there it is, whether we like it or not, and it is our lot in this ordained life. Zeal not for our own success, nor for the survival of every project or routine or even principle. Zeal to see God's glory shine brighter because of what we do in inglorious places and moments when perhaps nothing looks remotely shiny to us.

How odd that a pretty normal looking girl should sign up to be zealous about something that belongs in the spiritual realm, something so difficult to describe, something that lies in worlds beyond the one in which we live. How odd that dotted all over Scotland are zealots for something that would make most people feel just puzzled. It is glory and mystery together, and in this Easter season it is the most natural thing in the world to us.

Love to the Lord Jesus Christ... doing the kinds of things you do for someone you love to bits, the going-to-the-ends-of-the-earth things, the no-job-too-dirty things, the it's-not-about-you things, that you do for someone to whom you have given your heart. And what things you will do when it is for the love of Christ that you do them, because you'll do them in the lives of least and the last and the lost of this community and the whole earth.

We say a lot about Jesus' love for us. We sing a lot about our love for Jesus, though sometimes that can be a bit icky, especially if you have a 'cheese' threshold in hymnody that's set as low as mine is. But this vow is about showing that love by the thousand unsentimental duties of parish ministry, day after day after week after week after year after year.

Desire for the salvation of all... but you can't reach them all, or you'll do that minister-y thing and burn yourself out in no time. So, we come to places like this in moments like this and we find a great multitude of those who desire the salvation of all, and we share the task with all of them and with the crucified Christ, the risen Christ, the ascended Christ, the glorified Christ.

And we put away our mental lists of the people we particularly intended to serve, and see who turns up in front of us to inconvenience and challenge us. We might save them from physical danger: victims of war and famine, refugees and slaves. We might save them from society's dangers: survivors of domestic violence, young adults slithering into addiction or crime, teenagers being groomed and abused. We might save them in their spirits: those with the great decisions to make about their life's direction, those on their way into church membership or drifting out of it. And goodness, we make the salvation of all a possibility.

So far as you know your own heart... which genius in the Church's history thought to put something as unexpected as that into a vow (of all things)? But in that dim reflection in a grubby looking-glass, that is our understanding of our Christian faith, our ability even to be sure of our own hearts, to be sure how we will react in the best and worst of times, to be sure what will drive us forward and what will send us scampering backwards, is not guaranteed in the slightest. Whether you are faced with a marriage proposal, your own mortality, or a call to ordained ministry, you can only respond so far as you know your own heart. And God, and God's people, understand how uncertain that knowledge might be, and that's OK.

Your great motives... Like characters in a murder mystery, we live our Christian lives under the scrutiny of those who are probably wondering what we're up to and what we're trying to achieve, what has provoked us and produced such a rich response.

... and chief inducements to enter into this ministry. Well, x is not doing it for the irresistible salary! But I adore that phrase, chief inducements: it ranks glory, love and salvation above the things that seduce and induce us to be less than we ought to be. Those

things, for us ministers, include respect, visibility, influence, and probably a bit more respect for good measure. They must never be our chief inducements, and we need to be taken down a peg when it seems as if they are.

So here we are, in [...] on an April evening with Easter's light illuminating a fresh path for this people of this congregation. They will be drawn forward on this adventurous trail by zeal, love and desire, for glory, for their Lord, and for the salvation of the world.

Thanks be to God.

7 SERMON PREACHED AT THE ORDINATION OF ELDERS

Jesus said... Jesus said, according to John... Jesus said, allegedly, "I go to prepare a place for you". It is the most immense promise, and I don't think we claim it for ourselves.

I think we claim it for other people. It comes in the middle of the 14th chapter of John's Gospel, a passage that's used more often than not in funeral services, because of its words of comfort to bereaved people, and peace for our spirits. And if we pay attention to this astonishing promise at all, we are probably thinking about the person whose funeral we're attending, and take comfort that a place is prepared for him or her, so that they probably have a greater peace than we feel who are left behind.

But I suspect we don't claim the promise – that Jesus prepares a place for us – for ourselves very much. Isn't it rather an enormous offer to ignore, to fail to discuss, to fail to accept and relish and treasure and anticipate?

If a place is being prepared for you in a world better than this one, what do you need it to be like? Whatever little corner of the kingdom has your name on it, what do you need it to be like? Whatever is that place from which you never need to travel or progress again, what do you need it to be like?

Perhaps it needs to be peaceful, free of the aggression you may experience at the hands of others in the life you live just now. It needs to be peaceful, free of the ferocity of those in this life who won't notice hurting you to get what they want in wealth or relationships or reputation. It needs to be peaceful, with your broken loves resolved and your stupid arguments forgotten or at least forgiven.

Perhaps the place that is prepared for you needs to be unclouded, so that at last everything that stops you from seeing God is cleared away, and there God is after all. It needs to be unclouded, so that you understand what other people meant when you took offence and they really didn't mean to cause you pain. It needs to be unclouded, so you can understand whatever caused you confusion and anxiety in this life.

I've been watching a neighbour build a new house, and I pass it every morning on the dog's walk. It's been acquiring its roof-slates recently. And I can't help noticing that there are lots of complete slates lining up in tidy waterproof rows; but there have to be lots of differently shaped, differently-sized slates broken and split and chipped so that the corners of the roof, the junctions under the flashings, the openings for windows and flues, all have straight edges. There's lots of bashing and breaking going on to make a lovely new home.

I take every comfort from the idea that if all these Christian lives, including yours and mine, come together as if God is constructing a great building, then the broken-down slates, and the rubble infill, and the half-bricks on the ends of the walls, are all vital and no less important than any other piece of material.

The place that God is preparing is like that. People who seemed to live well and people who seemed to do terrible harm with their lives are built together. People who lived long and interesting lives and babies who never made it alive out of the womb are built together. People who changed the world and people who were only ever the victims of history are built together. People who relied on all-embracing love and people who managed to live loveless lives that just bruised everyone around them are built together. The place that is being prepared is maybe that place that is building us in with the bricks. My goodness – that is the place Christ is preparing, all along.

One of the best and most important things any minister or elder can do is put down the meeting-papers, halt the discussions about the building repairs, stop fretting about the annual accounts, forget for a bit the arrangements for the next formal communion, and instead prepare a place for people who need it and make them welcome there. There are people who need what I said earlier we need, a place that is very safe in a life that is full of risk, a place that is peaceful in a life too full of din and distress, a place that is unclouded and lets them see more clearly from lives that are a muddle. And of course we try to do that in part by making this place of worship such a desirable space, where we feel we are home and secure in the presence of the divine and welcomed by each other. But most of the people who are aching for a small corner in which their souls can thrive are not here in this place most of the time. So those who are asked to lead the Church are asked also to lead it outside the walls of its buildings, and create those safe spaces for people simply in our company, in the air of love and dignity and concern that we wear in our dealings with people.

And let's rejoice in the fact that the Church does this and does it well. The social capital of the Church, which is what you call the totality of the community ventures, weekday activities, involvement in wider society that the Church achieves, is colossal all across Scotland and beyond. Our job as individuals is to bring the same kind of blessing, one by one, to men and women and children who most need it, one by one. Being with us, being in our presence, should offer people something of that promise of Jesus to prepare a place for each one of them.

I may be an oddly-shaped roof-slate that looks a bit funny. You may be one of the least visible bits of guttering high up tucked under the eaves somewhere. The person next to you may be the most handsome block of stone right above the main entranceway, and good luck to them in that. We are built together to create a place, and then Christ offers that place to us, for now and for eternity, for the part of our journey we can see in this world and for the end of the journey we daren't contemplate most of the time. But Christ is the way to get there, so we may banish our fears, as leaders, as followers, as elders, as members, as strangers on the edge of the Christian community, wondering.

Thanks be to God.

Printed in Great Britain
by Amazon